2o

THE
Salesperson's
TIMETABLE PLANNER

THE

Salesperson's

TIMETABLE PLANNER

HAROLD L TAYLOR

KOGAN
PAGE

First published in Canada
in 1985 by Time Management Consultants Inc.
Second edition 1990.

This edition first published in Great Britain in
1992 by Kogan Page Ltd, 120 Pentonville Road,
London N1 9JN.

British Library Cataloguing in Publication Data

A CIP record for this book is available from the British Library.

ISBN 0–7494–0707–7

Typeset by DP Photosetting, Aylesbury, Bucks
Printed and bound in Great Britain by
Biddles Ltd, Guildford and King's Lynn

Contents

List of Figures

Introduction: The Value of Time

In no other profession is time management more important than in sales. A salesperson's greatest resource is the time available for customer contact. All the selling skills in the world are to no avail if there is not enough time in which to put those skills into practice.

A 1983 Canadian *Small Business Report* claimed that too much time was being spent by sales people on non-selling functions such as travelling, paperwork, waiting, etc. The typical salesforce distribution of time was described as follows:

- selling products or services   20%
- travelling, waiting, servicing   55%
- reports, correspondence, filing,
  administrative duties   25%

Time management for sales people should not involve rushing the sale, but reducing the amount of time spent on the other activities, thereby leaving more time for face-to-face selling. Time tips that work for manufacturing or finance people will also work for sales people. Everyone's time is valuable, but particularly the salesperson's time because it translates directly into increased income for the company and for the salesperson.

James F Bender, in *How to Sell Well*, reports that the seven most often mentioned weaknesses of sales people as identified by a life insurance company are as follows:

1. Failure to utilise time in work;
2. Failure to organise work;

3. Failure to plan work;
4. Failure to use enough selling time;
5. Failure to use enough product information;
6. Failure to use enough effort;
7. Failure to prospect for new business.

Many of these weaknesses would disappear if sales people would organise themselves and better use the time at their disposal.

Some sales managers note that out-of-town sales trips result in more calls per day and more sales than an equivalent amount of time spent in the home town. Could it be that time is managed more carefully out of town? There's no doubt that everyone is aware of the cost of travel, the limited amount of time available in that distant city, and the deadline imposed by the return ticket. There are also fewer distractions – little opportunity for friendly chit-chat over coffee, elongated lunches, trivial errands, or unnecessary phone calls. Out-of-town trips seem to have a sense of urgency attached to them, and an incentive to concentrate your effort. After all, it's not easy to make a repeat call the next day and carry on where you left off.

But the increased effectiveness out of town is probably due more to the planning. Calls and routes are planned well in advance; appointments are made and confirmed; time allotted to the calls is kept to a minimum to accommodate more calls; additional prospects are listed in the event of a last-minute cancellation or an abbreviated meeting; only prime, 'A' class prospects are included on the call list; the full day's 'selling time' is used; and preparation has been done the day or night before.

In other words, time is managed the way it *should* be managed. There is a tendency to lose respect for time when you're 'at home'. And if you don't respect your time, your customer or prospect certainly won't.

Next week, pretend you're *not* at home. Manage your time and territory as though you have only this one opportunity to reap the sales. Then compare the results.

If you feel that you need help to use your time more effectively whether at home or out of town, read this book, review it and apply it. You will find that time will be your ally, not your enemy.

CHAPTER 1
Get an Early Start

Morning momentum

The effectiveness of your day can be predicted within the first working hour. If you get off to a bad start – you're disorganised, tired, putting off calls, having that extra cup of coffee – then your day will probably follow suit. But if you are organised, if you have a daily goal, a plan and productive work habits, you will accomplish much.

Since the early hours of the morning are critical to the success of the day, the time to prepare your plan for those early hours is in the late afternoon or evening before. Don't leave the office until you have organised your desk and listed your objectives for the following day. Schedule your sales calls and other commitments in your daily planner. Resist the temptation to just walk away from the mess at closing time. Chances are, if you're disorganised when you leave at night, you'll be disorganised when you return the next morning. Psychologists have concluded that those who leave the office with a clear idea of what they want to accomplish the next day actually enjoy their personal lives more that evening. In contrast, those who leave with their desks and minds in a muddle, enjoy themselves less.

Try getting up earlier in the morning. You may be sleeping eight or more hours each night out of habit. If you need it, fine. But experiment first. If you sleep a half hour less each night, you'll gain an extra week each year. But more important, you'll get an early start on the day. You'll have time to review your day's plans, and to ask yourself whether what you had planned for that day will really lead you closer to your goals. You'll also have time to alter those plans if circumstances have changed in the meantime.

Most people report that their personal prime time is early in the morning. They feel at their peak – full of energy and enthusiasm – read to take on the world. Then their enthusiasm and energy wane as they experience the day's crises, problems and setbacks.

If you have more energy in the mornings, reserve that time for your priority tasks, whether they be sales presentations, writing, training or budget preparation. You may not be able to see many customers early in the morning, but at least schedule those high priority tasks that relate to your main work objectives for that day. Even if the rest of the day is fragmented by interruptions, telephone calls, meetings and rush jobs, you will at least have accomplished the important, high pay-off tasks. And you are more likely to do a good job if you are indeed an 'early person'.

Never leave important items until later in the day simply because you feel there may be more time then. Time always seem to dissipate faster as the day goes on. It's better to start a job and not complete it that day than never to start it at all.

The same thing applies to your personal life. Most people agree that exercise is more important than making beds, but we all know which activity gets the priority treatment.

Dive into the day

Some people go swimming an inch at a time. They stick a toe into the water and, shocked by the temperature, first immerse a foot, then two legs, followed by a torso. It's an agonising process. Each step into deeper water brings another cold shock to the warm body. Eventually they are totally immersed, and pleasantly surprised at how comfortable the water really is.

Many of us approach the day in the same way. We get up slowly, dawdle over a second cup of coffee, arrange our demonstration materials, procrastinate by first watering the plants, sharpening pencils, rearranging books, straightening our desk. An inch at a time, we ease ourselves into the day, only to discover that the jobs we dreaded were not that bad at all.

How much faster and easier it would be if we dived into the day as we would dive into a swimming pool, cutting out most of the preliminaries and getting on with the job at hand.

Surgeons take advantage of peak energy levels during early morning hours and schedule operations accordingly. If you are an 'early person', don't waste one minute of this valuable period of the day. Do your priority jobs first, and leave the morning newspaper, coffee ritual and desk-straightening until later.

One recent seminar attendee told me that he had to get up at 6.00 am to drive the distance to my time management seminar. 'What are you getting up at this hour for?' his wife had asked.

'To drive to Plymouth. I'm attending a seminar on time management,' he had explained.

'Well, if you got up this early every morning, you wouldn't *have* to go to a time management seminar,' she had responded.

And she was partly right. Early risers get a head start on life. They have the *opportunity* to get more accomplished during that relatively quiet time than they would if they arose in the midst of humanity's 'rush hour'. If you dawdle in the mornings and roll over for an extra 10 minutes' shut-eye, try changing your habits.

Build up some early morning momentum and you'll be able to coast through the day with less difficulty. Physics tells us that an object in motion tends to stay in motion and an object at rest tends to stay at rest. The same law applies to human endeavour. Overcome your daily inertia with a burst of early morning enthusiasm. Once you get rolling, you can plough through those daily tasks and achieve your daily objectives.

But above all, make sure you *have* daily objectives. Don't look at today as an extension of yesterday. Look upon it as an independent unit of time. Set daily goals that tie into your weekly, monthly and annual goals. Judge your performance on a daily basis. Before you retire each night determine whether you accomplished what you set out to do that morning.

CHAPTER 2
Stop Procrastinating

Why do we put things off? We realise that the present is all we have – that tomorrow may be too late. We are also aware that putting off today's tasks simply adds to tomorrow's burdens. And none of us wants to be one of those people who spends their whole life preparing to live and never getting around to enjoying each moment as it comes. Yet we procrastinate. Why?

Well, first we have to understand what procrastination really is. Some things have to be delayed; others should be delayed. But if we put off doing high-priority activities by doing low-priority ones instead, we are procrastinating. We straighten our desk, thin out our files and empty the wastebin instead of writing that letter to an irate customer. We sweep the patio, potter in the garden and smooth the kinks out of the garden hose rather than take the kids on an excursion. We thumb through magazines, read the paper and watch TV instead of getting started on that article we've always wanted to write.

Priorities differ from person to person. A kinkless garden hose may be more important to someone than exercise or recreation or family time. But we all know what our own priorities are. They are those meaningful activities which, when completed, give us a sense of achievement and satisfaction. They are the activities that help to attain those personal goals and desires which burn within us.

It is amazing how adept we are at thinking of other things to do when facing an important task. You would think that we would be enthusiastic about an activity that would produce gain, satisfaction and achievement. A long-term task, however, may not produce immediate satisfaction. We put it off, and focus on short-term tasks. We visualise the accomplishments we can make in the future but we tend not to recognise that few worthwhile things come without effort, inconvenience or discomfort. Our natural tendency is to avoid unpleasantness. So we sacrifice long-term benefits in favour of those minor, short-term rewards.

It's only natural to want to relax after dinner instead of washing up, even though the delayed task will be more difficult after the food stains have been allowed to harden. And who could fault us for leaving the broken stair unrepaired until the football game is over, even though it presents a safety hazard? And sleeping in on Sunday morning requires less effort than taking the family out. There is always a diversion at hand to make shirking our responsibility to others and ourselves more palatable.

Sometimes procrastination has minor consequences. At other times, it results in death, injury or unfulfilled lives. There is even the odd time that procrastination produces *favourable* results (and oh, how we love to rationalise our habit by recalling those occasions). But the habit of procrastination, regardless of the results, is self-defeating in the long run. It makes us feel guilty because we realize it's wrong. It is debilitating because we're constantly dreading the task that we are postponing. We're more tired mentally by not doing something than we would be physically if we were to do it.

The task we are postponing could be unpleasant in itself, such as weeding the garden – if we deem that unpleasant. Or its magnitude could be unpleasant. Writing a book could be overwhelming if we dwell on the length of time it would take. We tend to put off tasks that are either unpleasant, such as writing reports, doing the laundry, or making a cold call – or those that will take an overwhelming length of time, such as saving for a trip to America, finishing a recreation room, or prospecting for more clients.

To overcome the habit of procrastination, we must generate some enthusiasm to offset the unpleasantness. We must concentrate, not on the activity, but on the reward awaiting us upon completion. If the activity if unpleasant, let us pounce on it immediately and complete it so we won't have to dwell on its unpleasantness. If it's an overwhelming activity, let us chop it up into manageable chunks and polish it off a piece at a time. If we have to face a long road trip let's aim at driving six hours each day. If we have to produce year-end reports, let's aim at completing a proportion of them each day. If we have to pack the contents of a house in preparation for moving, let's aim at packing five cartons each day.

The hardest part of any job is starting. It requires great effort to get a loaded wheelbarrow in motion, but once moving, it tends to stay in motion. We are a lot like the wheelbarrow. Let's resolve to get started and let our momentum carry us on. Let's not wait for better conditions, a more suitable time, or better equipment. And let's not kid ourselves into thinking we need inspiration to do anything creative. Music critic Ernest Newman is claimed to have said that the greatest composer does not sit down to work because he's inspired, but becomes inspired because he is working.

Author Ari Kiev once wrote, 'When you postpone your involvement in something, you will probably never accomplish it, and will be left with memories of past wishes rather than past deeds'. Yesterday will never come again, and tomorrow may never arrive; but today is ours. Let's make the most of it.

There is always the odd task that is so overwhelming or distasteful that you keep putting it off *in spite of* your continued efforts to fight procrastination. You may even have scheduled it for a specific time or a specific day, but something more important 'mysteriously' arises at the last minute to pre-empt it. You need to be in top form to muster enough willpower to literally *attack* that task. More than early morning 'prime time' will give you. More than a motivated talk will give you.

But something *will* give you the power to attack that task and wipe it out. And that is *the power you get from having accomplished something significant*. How do you feel when you've succeeded in convincing the boss on a certain course of action, or sold a big order to a hard-nosed buyer, or received a promotion when several others were competing for the same position? Whenever you *succeed* at something, confidence and power well up inside you. You feel you can tackle anything. Use that power. That's the time to start that tough job you haven't had the heart to tackle. Attack it, and wipe it out.

CHAPTER 3
The Power of Planning

Plan before you act

No salesperson can be effective without adequate planning. Planning moves things from where they are now to where we want them to be in the future. It translates intention into action. Planning forces us to fill our diaries with the activities which reflect our goals in life. It protects us from all those trivial tasks that tend to obscure the important ones. And it prevents crises through foresight – recognising problem areas in advance and providing a course of action that will correct or eliminate them.

Planning ensures results. Many sales people have multiplied profits by setting aside Friday afternoon to plan their activities for the coming week. Others set aside the first hour of each day for this purpose. One well-known salesman claims he didn't succeed until he started planning his days.

Few of us deny that one hour spent planning saves three in execution. Yet we still don't have time to plan. And we don't have time to plan because we're caught up in the hectic, time-wasting activities that result from *not* planning. We're trapped in a vicious circle.

If you don't have time to stop and plan, there's only one solution – stop and plan anyway. Grit your teeth and let the world pass you by for a few hours. You may miss a few important calls, lose a few sales, antagonise a few people, but in the end you will save more time by planning than you stole in the first place. And your effectiveness will multiply. Schedule at least half an hour for planning each day, two hours each week, and four hours each month. Start with a statement of where you want to be, and work backwards from that goal. Don't start the morning by asking yourself, 'What do I have to do today?' That will only get you involved in activities. Instead, ask yourself, 'What am I attempting to *accomplish* today?' Everything should relate to your long-term objectives.

The higher up you are in an organisation, the further in advance you must plan. Cars trying to manoeuvre in a traffic jam would be analogous to a line person seeing only what lies immediately ahead. A lot of wrong moves can occur as a result of insufficient information, unless guided from above. First-line supervisors would parallel traffic helicopters radioing information to the cars based on a wider perspective of conditions below. Middle to top management could be likened to a plane flying high over the helicopter; a panoramic view of the scene below, surrounding territory, and distant landscapes allows management to give directions for an even better and faster route to a distant destination. Long-range planning is a roadmap to the future.

A good driver looks beyond the car in front, anticipates the possible actions of others, sizes up the traffic flow, heeds the radio reports, and proceeds along the best possible route. A poor driver keeps his eyes glued to the bumper in front of him and ends up crawling along behind a slow-moving truck.

Likewise, a good salesperson looks beyond the present day; he or she foresees future problems, makes detours to avoid traffic jams, and anticipates actions of others which could impede progress and productivity.

A good salesperson sets goals for the future, takes courses of action to achieve those goals, and measures his or her progress, not in terms of activity, but in terms of achievement relative to those goals.

Goal-setting and the planning necessary to reach those goals should be a daily process, not simply an annual event. One goal could be to complete a specific report by 9 am, to qualify three prospects by 10 am or to write six letters during a time scheduled for dealing with the post. The plans could involve such things as estimating the amount of time it would take for each activity, allowing for unscheduled interruptions or having telephone calls intercepted for that period of time; and gathering the necessary information in advance.

Larger tasks such as writing books, creating product brochures or designing a new layout would be handled the same way. But the larger the task, usually the more involved the planning becomes and the greater the amount of time that must be spent on the planning activity.

Annual goals involving sales increases, quality improvement and cost reductions would be broken down into monthly, weekly and perhaps even daily sub-goals which, when totalled, would become the annual goal.

Sales people who set goals and plan are more effective, more decisive, under less stress, less likely to get sidetracked, and are rewarded by the sense of achievement as each goal is reached.

Take a look at those jobs that are still to be done, set goals for their completion, establish whatever plans are necessary for their achievement, and not only will procrastination be a thing of the past but your personal productivity will climb.

Here's an example of how planning and goal-setting can result in increased sales.

When selling by telephone (or setting up appointments) keep track of every call you make. Keep a record of the person called and any relevant information gained from the conversation. If you actually get to talk to the right person, call that a 'completion'. If your percentage of 'completions' is not very high, work on your telephone technique in order to get past the 'screeners' with greater regularity.

From the 'completions', record those who could benefit from hearing about your product or service. These are your 'prospects'. Also keep a record of how many sales presentations you make to prospects each day, and how many of them result in sales.

Over a period you will accumulate statistics that can help you to set goals. You will be able to predict how many sales you will make based on the number of original calls, prospects and presentations. As your skills increase, these statistics should improve. The importance of time management will become more evident because your success will vary according to the amount of time you spend making calls.

The further ahead you can plan, the more effective you are as a salesperson. But don't neglect short-term performance. You can plan long-range, but you can't perform long-range. And doing is as important as planning. So translate your long-range and short-range plans into immediate activities. Fill your diary with those priority activities which will lead you to your goals. Leave only enough room for those last-minute emergencies. At the end of each day, determine whether you have accomplished what you set out to do in the morning.

CHAPTER 4
Scheduling for Results

Budget your time

Next to health, a salesperson's most valuable asset is time. It is more valuable than money. For money, like everything else, requires time to generate it. A salesperson must control the spending of time, and invest it in activities which will yield the greatest return. One way of assuring this is to prepare a 'time budget'.

A time budget is simply a plan for allocating time. It can be prepared by chopping up the day into segments, as illustrated overleaf.

Each segment is reserved for specific kinds of activity. For example, people who feel energetic and enthusiastic early in the morning should take advantage of this peak energy period by reserving it for more demanding, high-priority tasks. If possible, this should become the 'quiet hour' – a time free of calls and visitors. Appointments with class 'A' customers could be scheduled from 9.00 am to noon. Post and correspondence could be scheduled from 1.00 pm to 1.30 pm and so on.

The practice of performing the same types of task at the same time each day will reduce the brain's start-up time – the time it takes to get itself into gear and orientated to the tasks. It also allows the salesperson to make use of the natural breaks in the day (coffee break, lunch, closing time) as deadlines so that meetings and appointments don't engulf more than their allotted time. A time budget also ensures that 'prime time' is used effectively – for priority tasks – and that those routine activities are left for the late afternoon doldrums.

	8.00 am

Planning

Call preparation

	9.00 am

Priority sales calls

	12.00 noon

Lunch appointments

Post

Correspondence

Lunch

	1.30 pm

Sales calls

	3.00 pm

Prospecting

	4.00 pm

Meeting

Call-backs

Reports

	5.00 pm

Once a salesperson has established a time budget, he or she must stick to it as much as possible. It's only a plan, and deviations will occur. But these should be minimised. The salesperson must not make routine appointments, schedule meetings or become buried in paperwork during the 'prime selling' periods.

Next, you must schedule specific starting and stopping times for all your individual tasks or groups of tasks. It is not good enough to simply list 'priority tasks' and in the 'morning' section of your diary. If you have an hour to get ready for work in the morning, it will take you an hour. If you sleep in and you only have half an hour to get ready, it will only take you half an hour. It's a fact of life. Parkinson's Law tells us that work expands to fill the time available for it.

That is why it is so important to set deadlines for all your tasks and sales calls. If you just start writing that report or proposal with no idea of exactly when you plan to finish it, it will probably take you much longer than necessary. Instead, estimate how long it will take you, schedule that amount of time in your diary or day planner, and work towards that deadline. It will help if you schedule an appointment or lunch hour at the end of your time limit. A definite commitment to be somewhere else makes the deadline real.

Treat all your important activities this way. Draw up a plan of how you are going to spend the day and slot those tasks into the appropriate time blocks. But leave plenty of space in your diary. Don't schedule your entire day with no space for emergencies or sudden changes in priority. Schedule only those important activities which will lead you to your weekly, monthly and annual objectives.

Scheduling too many activities into your day is stressful and counterproductive. As the pressure of time mounts, we start rushing people, glancing at our watches and thinking of the other calls instead of paying attention to the one we're working on. When the people we deal with feel rushed they express themselves poorly, feel uncomfortable and get the impression we don't want to waste time on them. Results are rarely as good as they would be if we took the time for meaningful interaction. Instead of saving time, we simply alienate people.

Make sure that all the priority items of your 'to do list' are scheduled on your planning diary along with the meetings, appointments and lunch dates. Combine your 'to do list' with your planning diary and you will develop an actual schedule – a commitment – as to when you will perform each task.

The real priority items of your 'to do list' would appear this week on your diary, the lower priority items might not appear for two or more weeks, but each task would be scheduled for a specific time on a specific day. If someone should ask if you're free for a meeting on Thursday afternoon at 3.00 pm, the answer would be 'no' if you had an important sales call scheduled at that time.

The routine tasks should be broken down into daily 'to do lists' and recorded directly in your planning diary – but as a list above each day, not in any particular time frame. These are the items you peck away at during spare moments. If you misjudge the number of items you can accomplish in a day, you will still have to copy some on to the next day's schedule, but there shouldn't be many, for you have spread the items over several weeks. And hopefully you have allowed enough time for them. A good rule is to allow 25 per cent more time than you think it will take for each task or appointment. This will compensate for those uncontrollable interruptions.

A salesperson's prime time

Prime time for sales people does not necessarily coincide with their personal prime time (when they are at their peak energy level). Prime time is *selling time* – those hours during the day when they are able to contact the prospects and customers. If you're in sales, you cannot afford the luxury of waiting until you're feeling on top of the world before you venture forth to make a sale. If your prospects are available at 8.30 am, leave the paperwork until lunch time or after 4.30 pm when it's next to impossible to see clients.

Schedule your selling activities to correspond with your prospects' schedules, and perform all non-selling activities during 'non-prime time'. Don't leave for a sales call with a petrol tank that's almost empty, or with a tyre that has a slow puncture. Plan ahead. Changing a tyre, buying petrol, stopping for breakfast, setting up appointments, looking up telephone numbers, buying travel tickets, writing letters or having a haircut during prime selling time is counterproductive.

Prospecting time

Professional salespeople claim they must spend 15 to 20 per cent of their time prospecting just to offset the normal attrition of customers. Certainly, if all you do is service current customers you will eventually end up without any. Prospecting for new customers is a priority, and all priorities should be scheduled in your planning diary. So block off specific times in your weekly planner when you will go after those new accounts. Listing prospects on a 'things to do list' provides no commitment to make the call. Actually schedule several hours each week to contact those leads, introduce yourself and your product or service, and make appointments.

Make sure that all the necessary preparation, including looking up telephone numbers, qualifying the company or person as a prospect, digging up information on the prospect, line of business, current purchasing habits, credit rating, etc, is carried out during the non-selling hours when customers and prospects cannot be reached. Reserve prime time for the activity of selling.

Don't put off those sales reports

Call reports should be completed as soon as possible after the call. Don't allow them to accumulate until the weekend, by which time you will have to engage in creative writing to reconstruct a reasonable facsimile of your week's activities. Call reports are selling aids, not affidavits proving your activities. If you procrastinate, you will forget vital information that you spent precious time obtaining, information that could help to increase your sales.

There are plenty of five-minute chunks of time available during the day that would otherwise be wasted. Use it to complete those reports. Ideally, you will make notes *during* the call, and complete the report in your car *immediately following* the call. It's unlikely that your scheduling of calls is so precise as to

27

prevent a five-minute period for paperwork between them. Five minutes of paperwork is bearable, but after 30 calls, those two-and-a-half hours seem unbearable. Trying to reconstruct an accurate account can multiply that time to the point where you are overwhelmed by paperwork. A 'Customer Work Sheet/Call Report' form shown in Figure 6.5 (page 44), can be included in a sales binder or personal organiser and filled out before, during and immediately following a call.

Complete those reports while the event is fresh in your mind, and you'll actually save time. You're not stealing from your prime selling time – you're simply recycling time that would have been wasted otherwise.

CHAPTER 5
How to Use a Planning Diary

If you start work with a list of 10 items to do and stop at night with a list of 15, including the original 10, you may be a victim of the 'to do list' fallacy. A list of things to do provides no commitment to get them done.

Instead, separate the priority, high-payback activities from the items of lesser importance and schedule these 'must do' items directly into your planning diary as indicated previously. For example, a client proposal should never remain on a 'to do list'. Block out the time needed in your planner, let's say between 12.30 and 1.00 pm, and treat it as though it were a meeting with the client. Close your door and have calls intercepted, if that's what you would do if it *were* the client in person. But allow a little extra time for those unavoidable interruptions that are bound to occur. If you schedule several of these meetings with yourself during the week, you will accomplish those priority jobs and increase your effectiveness.

'To do lists' are fine for shopping, but if you're a profit-orientated salesperson, a scheduled commitment is a must. Be sure to set deadlines on all sales calls. Try not to overspend time on less important calls. It's difficult sometimes, but keep your mind on the objective of the call, not the activity of the call itself. When the objective is reached, the call is over.

Don't be discouraged if some of your scheduled activities have to be changed. A schedule is a guideline and must be flexible. But resist changing your schedule simply to accommodate tasks of no greater importance than your original, planned activity. Block off periods of time in your planning diary with the intent of following them through, but don't stop scheduling simply because your plans have to be altered frequently. Doctor's don't stop scheduling surgery appointments because they are often called out on emergencies.

The greatest example of commitment to scheduling was related by Mark Porter. Two busy mothers collided while driving their children to school one morning. They got out, inspected the damage, and decided they didn't have time for an accident right then. They agreed to meet later during their free time. That afternoon each woman drove to the scene of the accident, carefully manoeuvred her car into the exact position of the accident, and then called the police.

Myron Rush has talked about the time he flipped through his pocket diary, and suddenly realised he was reviewing the major actions and events of his life. He has a new awareness that time is the passing of life, and a greater respect for time.

This was only possible because he had *entered* his activities into his pocket diary. I recommend you use a larger planner than the pocket size and schedule activities and events such as birthdays and anniversaries; trips to be taken and holidays. Include rough maps of how to get to places and list items to take to sales meetings and conferences, etc. Then your planning diary will also serve as a record of where you have been and what you have done, complete with reusable information for the future.

Investigate the various types of planners on the market. Select one that has enough space for the entries yet is portable enough to toss into your briefcase. It should have time segments from 8.00 am to 8.00 pm or later (for recording personal commitments). It should contain the total year so you can plan well ahead and also have space for those daily 'things to do' that don't merit assignment to any particular time slot.

Figure 5.1 shows a typical time planner. It has all the necessary features and is the ideal size for photocopying your weekly plans for the office or boss. On page 34 are some tips on getting the maximum benefit from it.

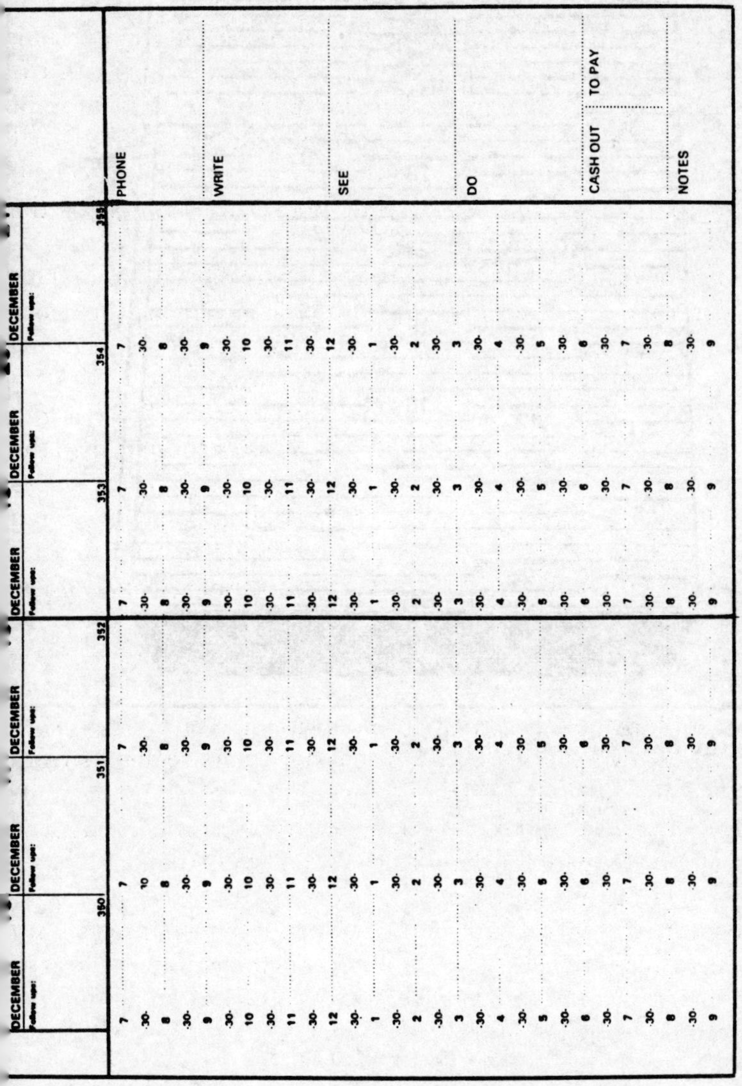

Figure 5.1 *Weekly time planner*

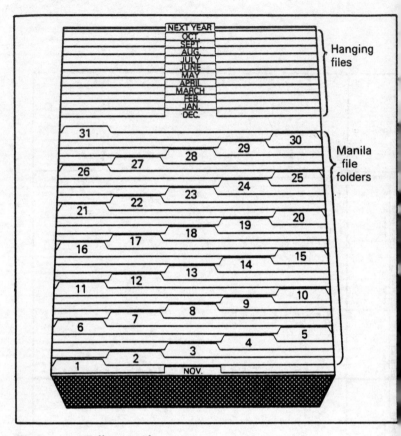

Figure 5.2 *Follow-up filing system*

A personal follow-up file contains the back-up material for those tasks and sales calls that you have scheduled into your planning diary. Nothing goes into this follow-up file unless a time to complete it has been blocked off in your planning diary.

The follow-up file system consists of 13 hanging files marked January, February etc, and the last one marked 'Next year'. One set of manila folders marked from 1 to 31, corresponding to the days of the month, is placed in the current month's hanging folder. If it's the first of the month and you have emptied the day's project papers, move the manila folder to the next month's hanging folder.

The follow-up file system is simply an adjunct to your planning diary. Your diary contains your work plan. If you arrive in the morning, flip it open, and see a call scheduled for 8.30 am, you know exactly where to look for the back-up papers needed for that call.

If *more* papers are received (related to a specific task scheduled for a future date), it's easy to locate the appropriate follow-up file folder. Simply flip through your planning diary to find the date on which that project is scheduled, and add the papers to the corresponding folder.

1. List your major goals in that section at the start of each week. Record only those that you feel you are able to accomplish that week. It's better to have only one or two major goals that will have an impact on your success than a long list of 'things to do' that rarely get done.

2. Make use of the daily 'follow-ups' section to highlight the most important call or visit that must be made on that particular day or the most important task that you *plan* to spend time on. In most cases, that task should be one that will help you to achieve one of your weekly goals.

3. Schedule time in the daily section to perform that major task or to make that important personal call. Treat them as you would appointments or meetings. Scheduling activities right in your planner will provide the commitment as well as the time to get them done. Beware of scheduling too many tasks in any one day. Leave plenty of room for those interruptions, emergencies and unavoidable delays.

4. Use the weekly to-do section to list those less important tasks that you would like to get done if you have time. This will include instant tasks, phone calls and follow-ups. Spread these minor tasks throughout the week. Be realistic or you will find yourself copying the same tasks into the next week's section. When listing people to phone, record the phone number at the same time; this saves looking it up later.

5. If you have a follow-up file mark 'FF' in the follow-ups section corresponding to the day you plan to follow up a letter, report, assignment etc. This will remind you to look into the follow-up file, and is an excellent way of keeping material off your desk until it's time to work on it. See Figure 5.2 for instructions on making up a follow-up file system.

6. Don't forget to record your personal commitments in the planner as well – football matches, theatre visits, dinners, etc. Make a note of them in the evening hours section. Be sure to record time and place of any social events, sports activities or meetings.

7. Put a sheet of self-adhesive coloured labels in the front pocket to mark important events such as birthdays, conferences, medical/dental appointments etc. At the end of the

year, you can use your current diary for reference and mark those same recruiting dates in next year's planner. It's almost impossible to miss an important date when a bright red dot screams out at you from the page. You can use different colours to differentiate between birthdays of family members, major clients etc. Place the label in the follow-ups section.

8. Stick a small pad of yellow Post-it notes on the inside front cover (use about one-third of the pad to reduce bulk). They come in handy. When a customer asks you to follow up on something or phone him or her with some information as soon as you get back to your office, write a reminder on a Post-it note and stick it on top of the scheduled task in your diary. You can't possibly forget. In fact, you won't be able to see what you have scheduled in that time slot until you *have* removed the note.

   Don't keep two diaries or you'll be trying to be in two places at the same time. If your office needs to know where you are, and what you have scheduled, photocopy your week's plan and leave it with your staff.

9. Keep an emergency supply of business cards in pockets at the front of the planner. Use the back pocket to store stamps, labels, memos, maps or other items used on a regular basis.

10. Record conference dates, meetings, holidays, business trips etc that are scheduled next year on the 'Year at a Glance' page as you find out about them. Don't ignore them simply because they're 'in the future'. You may need that information at any time. When you get next year's planner, schedule them into it immediately. Make sure you order your next planner no later than October of each year.

11. When scheduling meetings, trips, conferences etc in the DAILY section, record as much information as necessary including train or flight times, addresses, room numbers, and even instructions on how to get there. Little hand-sketched maps are useful if you have to return to the same place at some future date.

12. Retain all your planning diaries. You may want to refer to the information in years ahead. It's amazing how we tend to

forget those places we visited, people we met, things we did etc. Who knows, you may use them to write your autobiography some day!

CHAPTER 6
The Personal Organiser

I have developed a 'Personal Organiser' which has become my indispensable time management tool. It records everything as it occurs and reminds me as to what has yet to be done. It's a compact, 7½" × 10" portable, multi-ring binder with pockets in the front and back to hold business cards, labels, speedy memos, postage stamps etc. Three standard sections, described below, are separated with mylar-tabbed dividers and contain forms designed to keep you organised. Design one that suits your own needs or purchase one. You will eliminate misplaced messages or telephone numbers and follow-ups that might have slipped your memory. Here are three sections you should include:

Telephone and visitors' log

This section, which includes forms similar to the one shown in Figure 6.1, eliminates the need for all those scraps of paper which get misplaced, and it prevents you from having to rely on your memory after you have left a client's office or a caller has hung up. As you discuss business with a client on the telephone or in person, you record the name, company, nature of business discussed and any follow-ups required. The follow-up section is to the right of the form where it stands out. Once a follow-up is completed, a cross is put over that section. By flipping through the pages, you can tell at a glance whether any follow-ups have yet to be completed. It's a permanent record of any call or visit made or received, and the sheets can eventually be filed away as a diary or discarded once any relevant information, such as

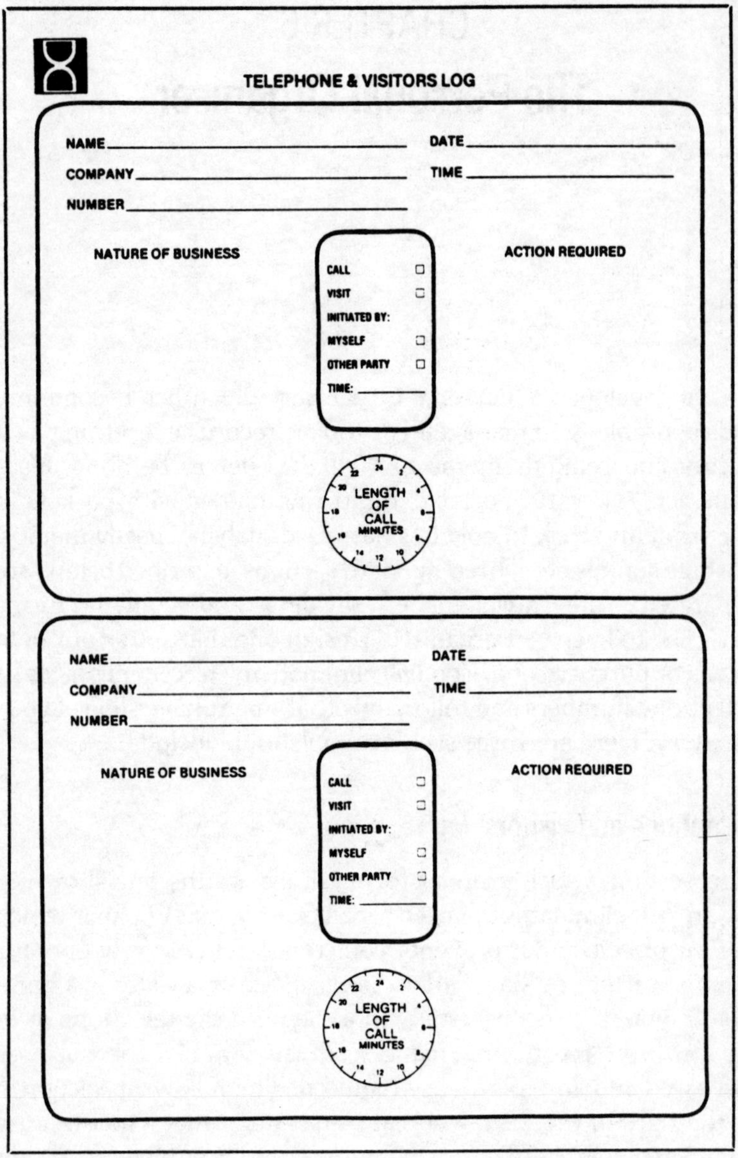

Figure 6.1 *Telephone and visitors' log*

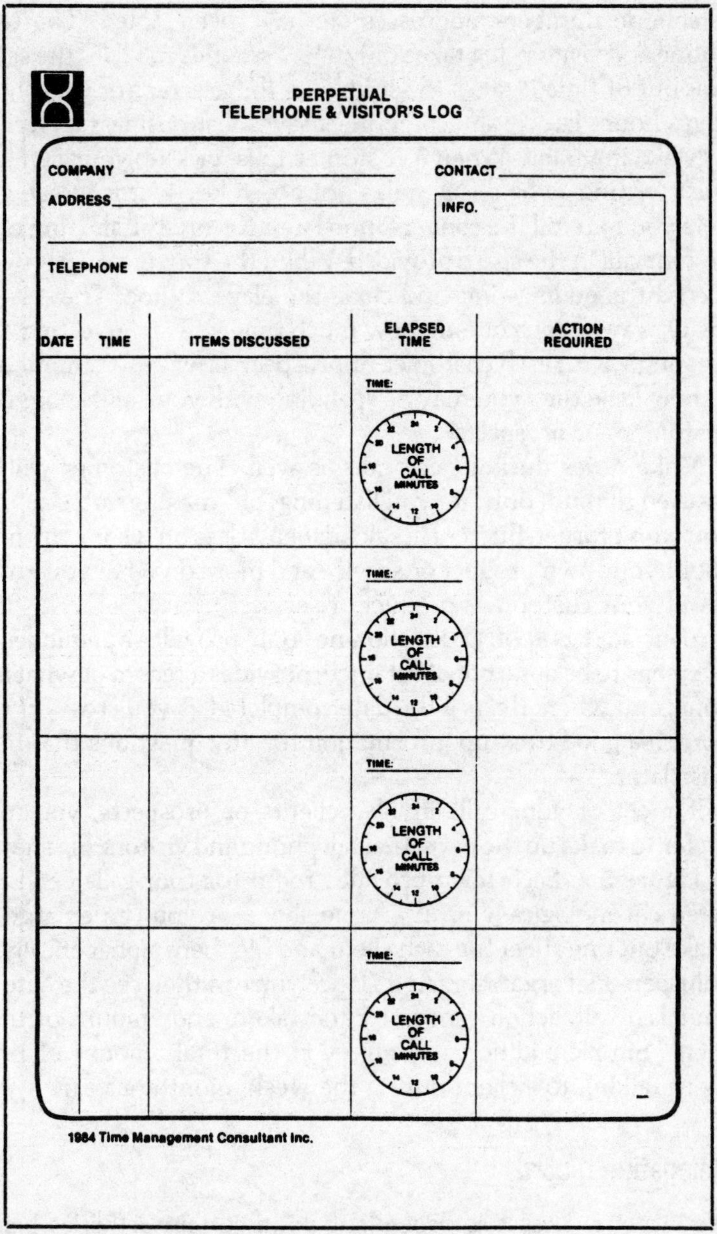

PERPETUAL
TELEPHONE & VISITOR'S LOG

COMPANY ______ CONTACT ______

ADDRESS ______ INFO.

TELEPHONE ______

DATE	TIME	ITEMS DISCUSSED	ELAPSED TIME	ACTION REQUIRED
			TIME: ______ LENGTH OF CALL MINUTES	
			TIME: ______ LENGTH OF CALL MINUTES	
			TIME: ______ LENGTH OF CALL MINUTES	
			TIME: ______ LENGTH OF CALL MINUTES	

1984 Time Management Consultant Inc.

Figure 6.2 *Perpetual telephone and visitors' log*

telephone numbers, addresses etc have been noted. The telephone and visitors' log takes only a few seconds to fill in (the same amount of time it takes to scribble on those scraps of paper) but saves hours later – and sometimes saves lost business as well.

Make it a habit. When a customer calls, pick up your pen and start writing as he or she talks. Jot down key words which will help you to recall the conversation later. Record the starting time of your call in the space provided. When the conversation is over, record the ending time and circle the elapsed time. There is no faster way of determining how much time you are investing – or wasting – with each customer or prospect. It will also remind you of how little time you may be spending with your high-potential customers or prospects.

Make notes during sales calls as well. The customer will be assured that not only are you listening, but making notes so that you won't forget. Success in sales depends less on what you know about your own product or service and more on what you know about your customer's product or service.

Your ACTION REQUIRED section not only provides a reminder of what has to be done but, if retained, provides a record of what *was* done, and when. Record the date completed as you cross off the note. It's good back-up information for any questions that may arise later.

If most of your calls involve clients or prospects, you may prefer to make up the perpetual telephone and visitors' log shown in Figure 6.2. Each form provides room for four calls or visits, listed chronologically on the same sheet, or you can enlarge it. Make out one sheet for each client and file them alphabetically in your personal organiser. At a glance you can then see the date of your last call, action requested and taken, and amount of time spent. Simple addition will give you the total amount of time spent talking to a client during the week, month or year.

Delegation record

When your success is dependent upon certain activities being performed by *other* people, it is important to keep a record of those items and follow them up before the agreed due date. The form

DELEGATION RECORD

MANAGER ______________________ MONTH ______________________

Date Assigned	Assignment	Due Date	Date Completed	Comments

"INSTANT" TASKS   Tick box at right when completed

Figure 6.3 *Delegation record*

The Salesperson's Timetable Planner

Name – Company – Address	Description and/or business	Telephone numbers
		Bus: Home:
		Bus: Home:
		Bus: Home:
		Bus: Home:
		Bus: Home:
		Bus: Home:
		Bus: Home:
		Bus: Home:
		Bus: Home:
		Bus: Home:
		Bus: Home:
		Bus: Home:
		Bus: Home:
		Bus: Home:

Figure 6.4 *Telephone index*

shown in Figure 6.3 provides such a record. Have one sheet for each person or department upon which you depend. Each time you make a request, record it along with the date promised. Glance at these forms each morning to see whether anything is due and follow up accordingly. It's bad enough when you don't receive information promised by a certain date; when you forget about it *yourself*, it can be disastrous. When you *do* receive the information or completed work, record that date. If a person or department is consistently falling short of expectations, you have all the documentation you need to take action.

On a more positive note, if some individuals are consistently fulfilling their promises and helping you to be more successful, this will also be recorded. And a word of appreciation will go a long way to ensuring that this cooperation continues.

Telephone index

Most telephone index books lack sufficient space, are cumbersome to carry, difficult to access or a bother to maintain. Or they are not around when you need them. Another section in your personal organiser solves the problem. Forms shown in Figure 6.4 can be filed alphabetically and added to as required. A separate column allows you to highlight the type of company, product or service handled, or other relevant information – for example, the names of an associate's children, a customer's birthday, time of day most readily available. With the additional information in this column you seldom fail to recall *why* that person is in your index. Over the years we tend to forget.

Since the personal organiser is carried with you wherever you go, you are never without access to the index. If one page fills up, simply add another. It is also easy to transfer numbers from your telephone and visitors' log to a permanent file. Pages can be revised with equal ease.

A telephone index should eliminate the necessity of keeping business cards. If you are reasonably certain you'll be using a number, record it in your index and throw away the business card. A hoard of business cards in your desk drawer is a time trap.

Other sections can easily be added to your personal organiser,

CUSTOMER WORK SHEET/CALL REPORT

Customer _____ Date _____

Address _____

Person contacted _____ Position _____

Telephone _____

Buying potential category _____ A ☐   B ☐   C ☐

Date last call made: _____

Call objectives: _____

_____

Customer's problems:	Benefits that will solve problems:	Features that will provide these benefits:

Opening remarks (promise of a profit improvement benefit):

_____

_____

Demands for justification anticipated:

_____

_____

_____

Closing questions to ensure accomplishment of call objectives:

_____

_____

Call analysis and next step to be taken:

_____

_____

Figure 6.5 *Customer work sheet/call report*

MEETING PARTICIPANT'S ACTION SHEET

NAME OF GROUP: _____ Date: _____

IN ATTENDANCE: _____

AGENDA ITEM	DECISION REACHED	ACTION REQUIRED	PERSON RESPONSIBLE	COMPLETION DATE

Figure 6.6 *Meeting participant's action sheet*

such as a 'Call Report' form (Figure 6.5) and a 'Meeting Participant's Action Sheet' (Figure 6.6) as well as lined paper. You may also want to keep such frequently used information as price lists, addresses and numbers of key prospects, holiday schedules etc in your binder.

Eliminate scraps of paper and avoid memory lapses, misplaced messages, and irate customers. Develop or buy a personal organiser and nothing will fall through the cracks.

CHAPTER 7
Use Idle Time

Don't wait to sell

If most sales people were asked why they bother waiting 20 or 30 minutes to see a prospect who is 'temporarily tied up', they might respond, 'You must be joking. If I don't see the prospect, I can't sell them anything!'

But they can't sell them anything from the reception area or waiting room, either. And are there no other prospects? Customers normally place very little value on a salesperson's time. After all, they're there for the customer's convenience. The customer is always right. Nothing happens until somebody sells something. Customers are the salesperson's bread and butter. Through these and other trite expressions, we are brainwashed into believing that our time is of little consequence when measured against the value of a possible sale. And the less value we appear to place on our time, the less value the prospect or customer places on our time as well.

The key to effective selling is to spend your time where it will do the most good. Face-to-face selling involves travel and waiting, paperwork and idle time, but don't spend 80 per cent of your time on customers who account for only 20 per cent of your sales. And don't waste as much time waiting for a prospect as you do trying to sell to him or her. If you make an appointment in advance, confirm it before leaving the office and arrive on time; you should not be expected to wait over 20 minutes once you arrive.

You may think that using waiting time on productive tasks, such as filling in report forms, reviewing sales literature and reading articles solves the problem. But it doesn't. Those things can be done during non-prime time. Prime time is when you are able to visit customers or prospects. It's unlikely you will be able to make appointments for 8.00 am or 12.30 or 4.30 pm, so use those times for your non-selling activities.

If you have set up the appointment properly, you will have agreed a time for the visit. After 15 minutes' waiting, you may not be able to do justice to the presentation in the time remaining. Politely convey this message to the customer via the secretary or receptionist, explaining that you have another appointment and will have to leave. If possible, ask for another time that would be convenient, schedule the new appoiontment in your diary, and be on your way. Make sure you reconfirm the appointment by telephone at the first opportunity, and apologise for having had to leave.

Be sure, also, that you have another prospect to call on! Always have some stand-by calls, either cold calls or customers that you know you can drop in on at a moment's notice. Phone them the moment you leave the tardy customer's plant or office, and explain the nature of your brief visit. Make sure you *have* a reason. Don't visit for the sake of visiting. Drop off a new product folder, explain a new service that might be of interest or, in the case of the new prospect, briefly tell him/her how your product or service could help his/her company.

An average salesperson spends less than a third of his or her time actually *selling*. Use that time wisely. And try to make more of it by reducing the amount of time spent in other activities – including waiting. If you *must* wait, be sure to use the waiting time for meaningful activities.

The waiting game

We wouldn't think of throwing away the small change in our pockets or purses. We collect it in a jar or piggy bank for lunch money, charity, holidays and so on. It's amazing how that small change adds up over time.

Yet we frequently throw away the spare minutes in a day – the pennies of time – by failing to use them.

Don't waste the minutes. Spend them on small tasks, such as reading, reviewing notes, memorising, writing a memo, organising a desk drawer or planning the next job.

Most of the minutes are wasted because we are caught unprepared. We never thought the plane would be delayed, or that we'd be kept waiting in a reception room, or that there would be a queue at the bank. Make up a 'waiting kit' and have it with you at all times. Use a portfolio, small attaché case, leather bag, manila envelope – anything that is easy to carry.

In it place some notepaper, pens, index cards and reading material. Add any filler jobs which must be done but are not urgent, such as a telephone index that needs updating, letters that need answering, or a cheque book that needs balancing.

Whenever you are faced unexpectedly with waiting time, dig into your waiting kit and put the minutes to good use. There are stories of people who wrote articles, and even novels, during these snatches of time on the underground, in waiting rooms or in queues. Longfellow translated the *Inferno* during ten-minute intervals while he waited for his kettle to boil. Harriet Beecher Stowe wrote *Uncle Tom's Cabin* in small segments of time between household chores.

You don't have to write a best-selling novel or learn a second language during the fragments of time you have available, but you can at least complete those petty little tasks that would normally consume your prime time. Use the minutes, and you'll have more to show for the hours.

If you carry your briefcase on business trips as well as to and from the office, convert it into 'an office away from the office'. Have all the essential items and materials for a productive work session at hand. Then, no delays, long waits, missed planes, travel time or time spent in hotel rooms will make you any less effective.

To organise your briefcase, buy a plastic folder (the kind with separate compartments) or a 'Travel Desk'. In it you should keep pens, pencils, magic markers, highlighters, scissors, tape measure, postage stamps, elastic bands, spare cassettes for your pocket recorder, a glue stick, miniature alarm clock, home address labels, small stapler, paperclips, staples, keys and coins. Add additional small items that you have discovered come in handy.

The 'Travel Desk' should fit easily into one side of a briefcase.

In the large pockets of your briefcase, keep a road map(s), writing paper, envelopes, notepad, promotional literature, blank self-adhesive labels and whatever else you find useful on a trip.

In the small pockets, include a small electronic calculator, business cards, travel tickets, passport and your favourite pen and pencil.

In the bottom portion of your briefcase keep some reading material, another notepad, your project or working files, and a cassette recorder. You will find that with a briefcase less than five inches thick, you will have room for all the above and more.

Organise your briefcase and you will find it will help to keep *you* organised. You'll be able to set up office in a train, plane, taxi, airport, hotel room or wherever you find yourself. Your waiting time and travel time can be productive – with few interruptions and distractions.

Let's assume you are 30 years old and your life expectancy is 80. Someone asks you how much you would want for four years of your life. You are shocked. There is no amount of money that is equal to four years of life. And as you get older you would be even more firm in your conviction.

Yet most people give away at least four years of their life and gain nothing in return. By wasting only two hours out of every 24-hour day, you will waste over four years during the next 50 years of your life.

We are horrified at the prospect of giving up four years, yet we think nothing of frittering it away a minute at a time. Take stock of yourself and your habits. When you're forced to play the waiting game, make sure the cards are stacked in your favour.

Education on wheels

The sales people who improve their track record the most are those who recognise that there's room for improvement. People who live on past accomplishments are has-beens; those who prepare for the future usually have a successful one. Learning is a never-ending process. You don't stop eating just because you have been well-fed in the past, so don't stop being educated simply because you have left school. Continually strive to excel by updating yourself on recent developments and theories, learning from other people's experiences, improving your skills, expanding your outlook, forming new habits, ridding yourself of non-productive habits, increasing your stamina, overcoming inertia and strengthening your self-motivation.

All this can be accomplished while driving from one place to another through the use of cassette tapes. The programmes available are unlimited. These are educational tapes, motivational tapes and self-improvement tapes. Best-selling books are condensed on cassettes. Interviews are recorded. Even the Bible is recited on cassette. There are condensations of best-selling novels, current events, live seminars and instructional tapes on almost every conceivable activity.

Look upon your car as your education centre. Have a cassette player installed if you don't already have one, or keep a portable player on the seat beside you. Collect tapes on various aspects of selling. Build a library of condensations of best-selling books. Purchase cassettes dealing with specific skills you wish to improve, such as effective listening, memory training, public speaking or creative thinking.

Do you have limited reading time? Then listen to those books you never had time to read. Buy cassettes of business books.

If you manage a sales force, build a resource centre of instructional tapes on all aspects of selling, from prospecting to closing the sale. Circulate them to your staff or issue cassette albums of self-study courses and periodically meet your sales force for group discussion and feedback.

Don't let that precious time spent in the car go to waste. Convert your car to a learning centre. Driving is usually done during prime selling time, and all prime time should be used for priority activities. Self-development is one priority that should not be overlooked. It could give you that winning edge.

CHAPTER 8
Don't Waste Other People's Time

Sometimes we are so intent on finding ways to avoid wasting our time that we ignore the fact that we may be wasting *other people's* time. One way to determine this is to ask the people who work with you on a regular basis. Be sincere. Explain that you are conducting a personal study to determine how you can help others to be more effective and would like to know if there is anything that you are doing that tends to waste their time. If open communication is encouraged, you may discover that you have been making unreasonable or unnecessary demands on staff and you can take steps to correct the situation.

A survey of personal executives by Accountemps in New York concluded that as much as one-third of every working day is being wasted. Replies to the survey indicated from 10 to 85 per cent of the 'work' day was spent *not working*. Regardless of the *actual* figure, it does confirm that there is terrific potential for productivity increases through effective use of time.

We sometimes spend more time wandering from one office to another then we spend in our own office. Are all these self-interruptions necessary? Mark Porter has related an incident which verified his suspicions that he wandered from his office unnecessarily. It seems that he tore his trousers, which abruptly forced him to change his habits. He stayed at his desk, accomplished more by telephone than by visitation, called meetings in *his* office – he even asked his boss to step in to see him. He wasted little time in friendly chit-chat, and at the end of the day discovered he had accomplished more work than he usually accomplished in a week. Because he had become desk-bound, he had been able to concentrate on his tasks. There's a lesson here for some of us.

There's a time for everything, and this includes socialising. If you are a salesperson, set the example. Be effective. Don't waste time. Socialise during the lunch hour and scheduled breaks, but *don't* lean against a wall or somebody's desk chattering away about the cricket scores or the current political situation. If you do, other members of your company will pick up the cue, and you'll soon be one happy (and non-productive) family. Remember, the name of the game is 'good' time management, not 'good time' management.

Most sales people blame *other people* for their time problems. Well, remember, *you* are everyone else's 'other people', so take a good look at your own habits. Do you interrupt your peers when *you* feel like socialising? Do you pick up the intercom or phone the same person several times during the day instead of accumulating the questions or ideas? Do you drag out telephone calls, visits or meetings?

Do you write letters when a phone call would do? Do you leave messages to call you back and then disappear from the office? Do you circulate junk mail with vague notations such as 'please note'? Do you give the secretary letters marked 'asap' instead of specifying a date? Do you leave the office without telling people when you'll be back? Are you a perfectionist? A procrastinator?

Don't drop in on clients unannounced to 'see how things are going'. You won't win any friends – or more sales – if you don't respect the customer's time. Make sure you have a reason to be there; a new product, service or idea that will help the client. And make sure you telephone first for an appointment.

Some sales people feel it's important to be visible so that the customer won't forget them. But it's better to be forgotten than to alienate the customer by making a nuisance of yourself. Fewer calls with more valuable information will reap greater rewards. If you feel you must keep your name in the customer's mind, you can do that with a quick telephone call asking if there's anything you can do to help out. Don't feel you have to pay a personal visit.

Take a good look at yourself. You may be someone else's time problem.

The sales call

Sales people have an obligation to use their time effectively, especially during a sales call. If they waste time during the sales call, they not only waste their own time, they waste the customer's time as well. And in addition, they try the customer's patience, temper and confidence. A poorly organised, unplanned, rambling presentation eliminates any inroads made by the company through advertising and direct mail, thus wasting the company's time *and* money. The prospects themselves may be missing a great opportunity to increase profits, cut costs or improve service. Everyone loses.

Surveys indicate that selling skills have increased dramatically during the last 20 years, while time management skills have remained the same. There are certain principles in conserving time just as there are basic principles in selling. They may not be applicable to all types of selling situation, but it may pay you to review them. In addition to reviewing the ideas presented in this book, I recommend that you read other books on the subject as well. A bibliography is given at the end of this book.

Use 'priority' selling

If the salesperson has planned ahead and prepared for the sales call, maximised the amount of time available for selling, and used any unavoidable idle time during the prime selling part of the day, the remaining time to be spent wisely is the sales call itself. If it's true that we should be spending most of our time on priority activities, then it's also true in the case of a sales call. Face-to-face selling is itself a priority activity, but within the time a salesperson is talking to a customer there is also an order of priority. *Asking for the order* has to be more important than the introduction. True, they're *all* important, but if you had 30 seconds to sell something, which part of the sales call would you select? The more often you can ask for the order, without antagonising the customer, the more likely you are to get it.

A salesperson should spend most of the time on the activity of greatest priority – the close. After a brief introduction and presentation you should ask for the order. The prospect may have been ready to buy before you arrived. If not, you should spend more time on the presentation – give some more benefits – and ask again. The old 80/20 rule probably applies here as well: 80 per cent of the results are obtained from 20 per cent of the time spent with the prospect. Make the most of the time you spend with a prospect. You can't be expected to 'sell' all the time, but don't waste that valuable 80 per cent on meaningless chit-chat that does not relate to your reason for being there.

Jack Kinder, Jr., Garry Kinder and Roger Staubach, in their book *Winning Strategies in Selling*, relate their practice of timing their actual face-to-face selling time. They recommend you place a stopwatch in your pocket and let it run whenever you're in the presence of a prospect, actually *talking about your product or service*. Don't let it run while you're driving, waiting or engaging in chit-chat. The accumulative 'selling' time during a week may be less than ten – even five – hours per week. The authors suggest you may not be earning the kind of money you could because you aren't spending enough time making calls. You may be putting in the hours, but not enough productive 'selling' hours.

The six-minute salesman

A successful publisher shared his secret of selling advertising space by saying that he was a six-minute salesman. The biggest hurdle was getting to see the prospect. He would do so by telling him he would only take six minutes of his time. Seven if he asked questions. The client was usually impressed. He didn't really believe the salesman, but this he had to see! When the appointed time came, the salesman would walk into the prospect's office, place his wristwatch on the desk and start right in.

The salesman claims the urgency of time put him in control of the meeting. It also forced him to pare down his presentation and make every word count. The prospect was also impressed, appreciated the respect being shown for his time, and generally took more than the minute himself asking questions. In fact, the prospect usually detained the salesman beyond 20 minutes – yet would not have been receptive if the salesman had *asked* for 20.

Respect for another person's time – and for time itself – produces results.

Sales people spend about 30 per cent of their time in face-to-face selling. The balance is consumed in travel, waiting, servicing and administration. Divide the total cost of supporting that salesperson by the number of hours of actual selling time and you will arrive at the hourly cost of selling. The resulting figure may shock you.

A six-minute salesman may be extreme, but it illustrates the point that selling time is costly and should be managed well. Prospects should be qualified in advance, appoiontments confirmed, presentations planned in advance, and emphasis placed on the priority part of the call – the close. A sale confirmed in 20 minutes is more profitable to the firm than one that takes two hours.

In addition to tightening up the sales call, the salesperson should attempt to gain more time for selling by reducing time spent in other areas. As mentioned previously, 20 years ago the number one problem identified by sales managers was the proper use of time. Today it's still the number one problem. Over the years selling skills have continued to improve, but there's no more time in which to use those skills.

We are all spendthrifts when it comes to time. We waste our time by spending a little here and a little there on trivial things that accomplish nothing. We reread a letter simply because it is complimentary. We glance at every piece of paper that is dropped on to our desk. We read items when we have no intention of responding yet. We daydream. We sort through the unopened post on the secretary's desk. We make unnecessary phone calls.

Time sifts through our fingers like sand through an hourglass – a few seconds here, a few minutes there – until we've lost an hour or more during the course of a day. An hour that could have been spent in face-to-face selling.

If you want to gain control of your own time, you must budget time carefully and put a stop to those hundreds of time leaks which plague everyone. Time management is the salesperson's responsibility.

CHAPTER 9
Managing Your Travel Time

Many sales people must travel extensively, and effective use of travel time becomes a major factor. If you are in this category, use a travel agent. Don't waste your time with engaged lines, being placed on hold, or trying to decipher the dozens of possible flight connections. A good travel agent can get you to your destination with a minimum of changes, stops and airport delays. Your travel agent should also open a file on you. This would include your normal form of payment, whether you are a smoker or non-smoker, seat preference, diet and car preference. Don't forget to ask the agent to sign you up for all the different airline mileage bonus programmes so that you can take advantage of free or discounted tickets on holiday trips.

A travel agent who takes a personal interest in your travel plans, anticipates your needs, and makes your trip as hassle-free as possible would certainly be an asset – and a timesaver.

Tell the agent what you expect. Specify direct flights where possible, connections involving a minimum delay, airports you would prefer to avoid. Where possible avoid arrivals and departures that coincide with local traffic rush hours. Book your tickets well in advance. And don't forget contingency flights in case you miss connections.

Arrive at the airport early for good seat selection. Remember, aisle seats usually have more space for hand luggage. Extra leg space is available in the front row of seats and at the emergency exits. Avoid the washroom area; it will get crowded on longer flights.

Always phone the hotel at your destination to reconfirm your room, making a note of your confirmation number and the name of the person issuing it. And check with the airline to find out if the flight is to leave on time. Make any arrangements for car rentals in advance. Use the agencies at the airports for convenience.

Photocopy your itinerary and leave copies with your office and spouse. Include such things as addresses and phone numbers of offices you will be visiting as well as the address and phone number of the hotel. While you're at it, photocopy your credit cards as well, just in case they get lost or stolen. It's faster than copying down all the numbers. Simply lay them out on a copying machine and photocopy both sides. Make several copies. Leave one with your office, one with your spouse, and carry one with you. If the embossed numbers don't come out clearly, rub a sheet of carbon paper over them.

If the meeting will keep you away from the office for several days, plan in advance the times you will phone the office so your secretary and co-workers can have their questions and important information at their fingertips. Otherwise it might be a fruitless, frustrating, time-wasting exercise. Also let them know what to expect during your absence.

When packing, save space. Where possible, limit yourself to hand luggage to avoid waiting at the luggage carousel. A lightweight vinyl saddlebag that slips over your briefcase (Figure 9.1) is ideal. Five compartments hold everything from shirts and blouses to trousers, socks and a portable hairdryer. Everything is carried in one hand, leaving the other free. Once on the plane, simply slip off the saddlebag and place it on the overhead rack, and slide the briefcase under your seat, ready for use.

If you travel often, one or more of these compartments can remain packed with personal items to eliminate the necessity of collecting and packing them every time you take a trip. Or keep a tote bag fully stocked with all the personal items you normally use at home. This is not to be used except when travelling. Pack it into your suitcase whenever you travel and you never have to worry about forgetting your toothbrush, miniature sewing kit or nailclippers. To make one up, buy a duplicate of everything you use in the morning and place it in the bag. Then work from that

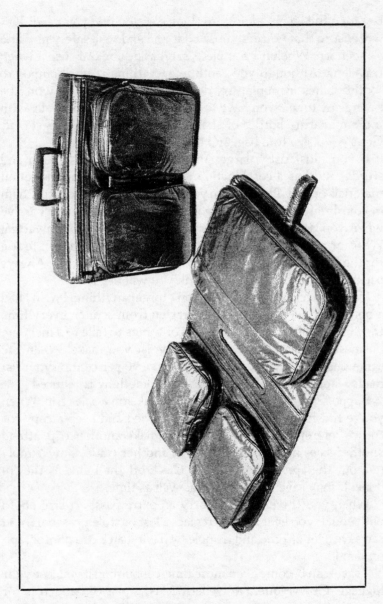

Figure 9.1 *Traveller's saddlebag*

bag for a full week, adding anything else you find you need. This will ensure that you add those odds and ends like safety pins and a shoehorn. When it's complete, set it aside and only use it when travelling. Although you can buy everything from shampoo to toothbrushes in miniature, don't go overboard. You won't be saving any time if you have to replenish your kit repeatedly with more miniature bottles of shampoo, aftershave, toothpaste etc. Get a good size tote bag, and live in luxury!

If you must use a large suitcase, make sure it's tough and sturdy, and has a combination lock. Don't pack demonstration materials or sales literature in your suitcase. Make room for them in your briefcase or hand luggage. If your suitcase doesn't arrive when you do, at least the purpose of the trip is not thwarted. Wear (or pack in your hand luggage) the clothes you plan to use for the first sales call in case your suitcase is late arriving. Always pack fewer clothes than you think you will need.

Have a checklist so that you won't forget anything. I wish I had a pound for every person who started from scratch every time they made a list. I mean those lists of things to take to a meeting, business trip, and so on. Keep every list you make. When the same sales trip recurs, you already have 90 per cent of your list made – and the likelihood of missing something is reduced.

Suppose you make a list of items to take on a sales trip. When you're finished with it, have the list typed and keep a copy for future reference. When you have to make another trip, attend another sales meeting or exhibit at another trade show, simply pull out the appropriate list and check off the items as they're done. It may save a lot of grief as well as time.

When you travel abroad, carry an extra passport-size photo with you. If you ever need to replace a lost or stolen passport, you can save a lot of time and trouble by having an extra photograph on hand.

Travel can become even more time-consuming if you lose your luggage. One frequent traveller packed a pair of handcuffs for securing luggage to airport railings during long waits for planes. This may seem a bit excessive for most people, but here are some practical tips to keep the possibility of loss to a minimum, and if it *is* lost, to get it back to you faster.

1. Remove all old airline tags that might cause your suitcase to be misdirected.
2. Keep a business card *inside* as well as outside your suitcase in case outside identification gets pulled off.
3. Identify your destination – name and address of the hotel on the card inside.
4. Do not overpack or it might spring open. And lock your suitcase.
5. Stick coloured labels or other distinctive markings on the suitcase for easy identification.
6. When checking your suitcase, make sure it's tagged for the correct destination.
7. Never leave your suitcase unattended.
8. When arriving at your destination go immediately to the baggage reclaim area.
9. If your case doesn't arrive when you do, report it immediately.
10. In spite of precautions, there is always the possibility you will arrive at the hotel *without* it. So it pays to have hand luggage with you containing what you need immediately, including what you intend to wear at your first meeting.

An organised briefcase is essential, since you'll have plenty of opportunities to work on priority tasks in a train, taxi, airport, plane or hotel room. Make sure you have all the essential items to hand.

Organise your work projects as well. Use coloured folders labelled 'To Do', 'To Read', 'To Phone' etc. A small cassette recorder is ideal for dictating letters, ideas and call reports, and information picked up during sales calls or at meetings.

Arrange your trip so you can use this organised briefcase to work on priority projects. Take a taxi or hire car to the airport so that you can deal with paperwork en route. You conserve time and energy by not having to find a parking space and making the long trek with a briefcase and luggage to the proper departure area. Select a seat with room for your briefcase underneath, and work on priority material early in the flight while you're at your peak. Leave reading material and routine paperwork for times when you're feeling sluggish. Always relax just before touch-down and don't fight the crowds when disembarking. Relax. If you have luggage to retrieve, you'll be waiting anyway.

If you don't need a car at your destination, don't hire one. Save time and effort by taking taxis. Avoid the airport buses. They're usually late, uncomfortable and not conducive to either reading or resting. If your meeting can be scheduled at the airport hotel, better still.

On arrival at your hotel, review your itinerary and use your time wisely. You have some excellent uninterrupted time at your disposal. Use the desk in your hotel room. Order room service instead of using the coffee lounge, and knock off a few letters or a report while waiting for it to arrive. Take advantage of meeting delays or waiting time to work on those 'to do' items. Plan to return to the office with the trip follow-ups and paperwork already completed.

To keep track of the cost of business lunches, dinners and other expenses, jot down the details on your credit card receipt at the time you sign it. This will prevent you from forgetting later. A daily expenses diary is also a good idea – and a timesaver. Know in advance where you're going to stash all those receipts you will need for your expenses report later. A good place is in your airline ticket folder, or keep an envelope in your jacket pocket or handbag. A little organisation during the trip will save time (and prevent missing receipts) later.

With travel costs increasing and time at a premium, the mark of an effective salesperson is how well he or she manages time away from the home office.

In the car

If a salesperson works eight hours per day, and drives 10,000 miles in a year at 40 mph, he or she spends over 31 days travelling. If there are 10 sales people travellling the same 10,000 miles, the company is paying the equivalent of another sales person just to cover the travel time.

Unfortunately, we can't simply beam ourselves to our destination in Star Trek fashion. But what we can do is to use our own travel time more effectively and encourage others to do likewise. Once the territory has been designed to minimise travelling time, there are still several ways of productivity using the time spent behind the wheel.

Professional development
There are some excellent cassette tapes available – everything from condensations of best-selling books to motivational and sales training tapes. This is far more productive than listening to the same news over and over again on the radio. And it can reap benefits in terms of professional development.

Dictation
Letters, reports, sales quotes, follow-up lists and ideas can all be dictated into a small pocket recorder while driving. This will reduce the time normally spent on paperwork later. It also prevents you from forgetting those creative ideas that seem to pop up out of nowhere.

Planning
Driving time can be used for planning the day, rehearsing a presentation, solving a problem or reviewing and evaluating the day's activities. To be effective, however, you must be able to discipline yourself. Your mind has a tendency to wander away and engage in a little extra-curricular daydreaming.

Relaxation
Don't forget that on certain occasions you should do nothing except relax and listen to music. It clears the head after a particularly hectic morning. A relaxation break is productive when it revitalises you for the tasks ahead.

Quiet hour
During a heavy traffic build-up or when a long drive has made you particularly weary, you should consider pulling off the road and setting up office for an hour. In fact it might be a good idea to make a habit every day – perhaps while you're still in a client's

car park. Your briefcase should be equipped with everything you need to schedule your next day's clients, summarise reports and statistics, update your log book. This 'quiet hour' in the car ensures interruption-free time away from the hustle and bustle of the office. Unencumbered with telephone interruptions and visitors, your paperwork can be dispensed with quickly. Be sure you don't waste prime selling time, though. Use those times of the day when you are unable to see clients.

Here are a few more hints on saving time while on the road:

1. Plan your travel route in advance. Make sure your latest calls are closest to your home or office. You will waste less time sitting in rush-hour traffic.
2. Use a checklist to ensure that you have everything you need for the trip, including change for pay telephones, addresses and phone numbers, spare ignition key. Think the trip through chronologically as you make the list so that you don't forget anything.
3. Be sure to take reading material with you for those inevitable waits in reception rooms.
4. Keep a record of all your calls. List what went right, what went wrong, follow-ups required, problems to be solved. And do it immediately following the call. Don't leave it until you get back to the office. Relying on your memory can be a major time-waster.
5. If you have to travel a considerable distance to make one call, research other prospects you can visit while in the area. You'll reduce the travel time per call.

The average salesperson spends less than 30 per cent of his or her time in front of prospects, while travelling and waiting take up at least this much time. Just think what the results would be if face-to-face selling time could be increased to 50 per cent. This could be accomplished easily if travel and waiting time were used to dictate letters and reports, dispense with paperwork, plan, summarise sales calls, listen to tapes, and anything else that must be done.

Time is the ultimate money. Everyone has the same amount – no more, no less. How effective we are as sales managers or sales people depends on how we use it.

CHAPTER 10
Meal-time Meetings

Breakfast meetings

Business lunches tend to soak up time like a sponge soaks up water and yet they are a normal part of a salesperson's life. If you have problems with meetings that take too long, try a breakfast meeting. By starting early, your clients miss the traffic jams, are normally at their mental peak, and will probably be anxious to get the meeting over with so they can get started at their regular jobs. There will also be few, if any, interruptions if held before office hours. The incentive for starting early could be a nourishing breakfast. It's the healthiest meal of the day, and beats liquid lunches. An added advantage of a morning meeting is the opportunity to follow up immediately on the important items.

Be sure to start early enough to gain the advantage of silent telephones. Set a deadline, keep the meeting brief, and discuss business over coffee. Don't hold the meetings too often. After all, you are using up most people's prime time in order to have them and if they're not essential and effective, you'll have a revolt on your hands.

The business breakfast is gaining popularity as a timesaver. Here's a summary of the major advantages:

1. They don't interrupt the day's work, are normally shorter, and are easier to walk away from ('It's almost nine – I must dash').
2. People are usually more objective after a good night's sleep. They are more patient. And most of them are in their prime time of the day – wide awake, enthusiastic and creative.

3. They are less expensive than taking clients or business associates to lunch or dinner.
4. There are usually no phones, less food to wrestle with, and no temptation to order mind-deadening drinks.
5. If there is action to be taken as a result of the meeting, people have all day to do it. In fact, it's a good time of the day to get on someone else's 'to do list'.
6. Breakfast meetings provide a good 'neutral' location, away from the office and its formal atmosphere.
7. As a replacement for those dinner meetings, the early morning meetings contribute to keeping family time intact.

If you're having a breakfast meeting, you might as well use the opportunity to make it nourishing. Stay away from continental breakfasts. If you're in a hurry, try a protein breakfast such as yogurt, muesli with skimmed milk or orange juice and cottage cheese. Sweet breakfasts consisting of refined sugar and starches will cause your blood sugar to rise sharply. Insulin is introduced into your system, causing your blood sugar to fall and your emotions to fly.

It makes sense to use the meeting as an excuse to have a really good breakfast, because it is the most important meal of the day. It has been claimed that people who eat breakfast live longer than the ones who skip it. A breakfast supplying about 20 grams of protein might consist of two eggs, a glass of milk, a slice of wholewheat bread and some fresh fruit.

Business lunches

Unlike breakfast meetings, business lunches tend to drag on and are largely ineffective – although some people claim they remove the pressure of social visits in the office. If you must hold meetings that run through the lunch hour, be careful. One manager, after a big lunch, dreamed he was chairing a meeting, and then woke up to find out that he was. Keep the food to a minimum and limit the alcohol. Sandwiches and cold buffet will keep you from starving. Roast beef and Yorkshire pudding will keep you from remaining alert.

Occasionally you may have to hold a business meeting during the lunch hour because of time restrictions or at a client's request. Try not to make complicated sales presentations or discuss detailed financial matters. Those items should be handled in advance. The atmosphere of a restaurant is just not suited to anything more than general discussions. But make it as quiet as possible by reserving in advance and requesting a quiet spot – if one exists. If you're meeting the others there, arrive early enough to pick a table far removed from the entrance and kitchen and with enough lighting to avoid eyestrain. Make your guests as comfortable as possible by commenting on any of the menu items you have tried before. Speak up when the waiter asks if anyone would like a drink; otherwise there's an awkward pause while everyone tries to guess the appropriate response. Invite the others to make their choice, then quickly order something light. Alcohol at lunch time can be counterproductive so I suggest mineral water. Even though the maxim states that you should eat like a 'king at breakfast, a prince at noon, and a pauper at night', big meals at midday can make you sluggish in the afternoon. If you want to maintain your momentum, eat lightly, and especially stay away from alcoholic beverages. Unleash your hearty appetite at dinner time, when it won't affect your personal productivity.

Fruit juices and mineral water in many cases are replacing alcohol in popularity. Milk, yogurt, fish, fruit, cottage cheese and other nutritional items are being ordered in place of the meat and two veg. The low-calorie salad bar is gaining ground. Those who persist in calling salads 'rabbit food' should remember that rabbits never develop heart disease.

Don't start discussing business until the orders have been taken, and avoid circulating reams of paper or trying to take copious notes. When the food arrives, switch the conversation away from business except to summarise what has already been agreed.

Try to avoid any fumbling or embarrassment at the end by telling your clients at the start they are your guests. And let the waiter know in *advance* that you will be getting the bill.

Robert Townsend, former Avis CEO and author of *Up the*

Organisation and *Further Up the Organisation*, describes the perfect business lunch as one that never happens. He feels that lunch is no time to discuss important matters, claiming that it could take two hours in a restaurant to discuss something that could be completed in half an hour in the office. Other business leaders share Mr Townsend's opinion. If you *do* hold business lunches, make sure the results justify the expenditure of time.

And at least consider joining the soda and salad group who start the day at the local fitness centre. Breakfast meetings fit in better with the trend towards a healthier lifestyle. And who knows, you may even start enjoying that hearty, energy-producing breakfast that you never had time to eat before.

CHAPTER 11
Manage Your Telephone

Prime time for telephone calls

It has been reported that the average sales representative in the fields of property, insurance and securities wastes as much as 80 per cent of his or her selling time. Personal visits involve problems such as traffic hold-ups, long waits in reception rooms and broken appointments. The point is made that proper use of the telephone can save time and increase sales.

You may not be able to sell your product by telephone, but you can certainly save a lot of time qualifying your prospects by using the telephone to set up appointments. Assuming the same closing rate, doubling the amount of face-to-face selling time will double your sales. Getting to see the right person can be a time-consuming venture unless you obtain all the information in advance and make an appointment via the telephone. Use the telephone wisely and sales will increase.

Some people are always 'tied up' or 'in a meeting' first thing in the morning. Others are unavailable in the late afternoon. Some may be reached easily between 11.00 am and noon. It varies with the individual because not everyone schedules their time the same way. In some cases, a person may *always* be unavailable because they have all their calls screened.

Time is frequently wasted in attempting to get in touch with people because their prime time for telephone calls varies. So make a point of finding out the best time to call people, and record that information along with their names in your telephone index. Don't be afraid to ask. A simple, 'What's the best time of the day to get hold of you, Charlie?' may result in some valuable information. Charlie may tell you he's always out of the office on Mondays, or is always tied up in the morning before 10.00 am, or usually uses the lunch hour to return calls.

Similar information may be available from the person's secretary. So if you fail to reach someone on your first attempt, always ask the secretary for the best time to call back. If you want the other person to call you back, make sure you tell the secretary when *you* can be reached as well.

The important thing is to recognise that times vary for different professions and different individuals.

Get maximum value from your telephone

You should take advantage of the telephone to avoid excessive letter writing and time devoted to meetings and visits. If someone wants to see you, or wants you to see him, try to settle the matter on the phone. Consider using conference calls to avoid costly meetings. Use the telephone to provide answers to written queries. Investigate the various equipment options available: a speaker telephone to free your hands for work, flashing lights to avoid the nerve-jangling and disrupting bell, automatic dialling to save time looking up numbers. Remember that the telephone is there to serve you, not the reverse. Control it. Don't be a slave to it. And you'll be more effective as a salesperson.

Have you ever considered the total time that could be saved if all the calls ever made were reduced in length by only one minute each? Of course, we can't control other people's calls. But if we reduced our own 1000 calls by one minute, we would save the equivalent of over two full working days. A minute is important when there are so many of them! Here are some suggestions for improving your use of the telephone:

1. Don't be a slave to your telephone. You're not expected to be at its beck and call. Have calls screened during certain 'quiet hours' when you want to work on priority tasks. If you have no one to screen your calls, get an answering service. You

can't be effective while constantly reaching for the telephone. Try not to schedule these 'quiet hours' during prime selling time, however.

2. Be polite, but brief. The way you use the telephone at home should be different from the way you use it at work. Its prime purpose at work is not for socialising. When Jack calls, answer cheerfully, 'Jack, what can I do for you?' It's not impolite, but it brings the caller to the point a lot faster. When *you* call, don't assume the person has time for chitchat. Get right to the point: 'The reason I called, Mr. Wilson . . .'

3. Control the conversation. In meetings, a chairperson controls the conversation and keeps it on course. Appoint yourself chairperson, and direct the conversation to the objective of the call. Like a meeting, once the objective is reached, the call is over. End it politely, but promptly.

4. Group the call-backs. Get in the habit of accumulating your messages and returning the calls in a group. Just before noon is a good time, because conversations tend to be briefer when they threaten to interfere with lunch. About 4.30 pm is a good time to return the afternoon calls.

5. Dial your own numbers. It takes just as much of your time to get the secretary to place your calls as it does to make them yourself. With touch-tone telephone, direct dialling, telephone rests and routine 'filler' work, even the engaged tone won't result in much lost time. So why waste your secretary's time? His or her salary comes out of the same pocket.

6. Record the best time of the day or week to reach the people you telephone on a regular basis. Include this information in your telephone index.

7. If you want to get through to the boss, try calling before 9.00 am or just about 5.00 pm. The boss will probably be there, especially in smaller companies. But be careful you don't become a nuisance.

8. Consider an automatic dialler. It not only saves time in dialling, but saves time otherwise spent looking up telephone numbers (those numbers of relatives, friends and business associates that you don't use frequently enough to memo-

rise). The number of programmable telephone numbers varies with the model, but you can usually accommodate those emergency numbers as well. And there's nothing faster than pressing a button.

9. Install touch-tone telephones. It takes at least four times as long to dial using conventional telephones. Keep up to date on telephone technology.

10. Don't get in the habit of holding longer than a few minutes unless you have a lot of routine work you can do while you wait. Leave a message instead.

11. Before making a call, quickly jot down the points you want to raise so that you don't forget anything. If you have several questions to ask or points to make, announce this at the start. 'There are three items I'd like you to consider, John . . .'

12. If the person you're calling is not there, try to get the information you need from someone else rather than leave a message to call back.

13. If you have a secretary, ask her to intercept incoming calls and handle them when possible. Also ask your secretary to return the calls that he or she can handle.

14. When your secretary takes messages, make sure he or she records what the call is about and records the telephone number so that you don't have to look it up.

15. If someone calls for an appointment, try to settle the business right then, and avoid a time-consuming meeting.

16. When possible, arrange your call-backs in order of importance in case you're interrupted before you finish.

17. Always have routine jobs available (signing letters, filing etc) to fill waiting time when making a series of calls.

18. If some callers are long-winded, try letting them talk themselves out. Silence tends to end a conversation sooner. This is practical only when you have routine jobs to perform while listening.

19. If you have already agreed to meet the caller, don't waste time discussing the business on the telephone as well.

20. If you have a gossip on the other end of the line, excuse yourself by being frank about your time problem.

21. If you need information to allow you to work on your

priority items, make those calls early in the morning to get on that person's 'to do list' for the day.

22. Make notes on all calls. They're just as important as meetings, and you probably have some things to follow up as a result of them. Don't rely on your memory.

23. Ask your secretary to pin your telephone messages on a cork board on the wall at your side. You can easily pick out the important ones at a glance. This will only work if you keep a clear board at all times. Don't let them accumulate.

24. Don't be afraid to say 'goodbye'. Take the initiative to control the length of the call. 'Well, I'd better let you go, I know you're busy.'

25. When leaving a message for someone to return your call, be sure to get the name of the person taking the message. It gives you a name to refer to the next time you call, improves interpersonal relations, *and* it increases the likelihood that your party will get the message.

26. If you have an automatic telephone answering device, don't leave too much time between the end of your instructions and the 'sound of the beep'. People in general dislike talking to a machine. Give them too much time to think it over, and they'll hang up. One executive reported that reducing the length of the pause from 14 to 8 seconds reduced hang-ups to practically nil.

27. Get into the habit of spelling out exactly when you will be calling someone instead of a loose, 'I'll ring you on Friday'. Treat it as you would a personal appointment or meeting. Agree on a specific time, length of call, and record it in your planning diary. This will avoid lost time trying to get hold of the other party or forgetting the 'telephone appointment' altogether.

28. Identify yourself right at the start. Don't force the secretary to ask who's calling.

29. When you reach your party, ask if it's convenient to talk now. Remember, you have interrupted this person by your call.

30. State the reason for your call. Don't waste time on introductory chit-chat. Start the conversation by recognising you're

infringing on his or her time. 'Sorry to interrupt you, Susan . . .'

31. Don't become so involved in signing cheques, filing or other activities while talking, that you miss something.

32. Don't try to carry on side conversations with gestures as you talk on the telephone. Ignore people who try to get your attention or push papers in front of you for signing.

33. Force yourself to concentrate on what the other party is saying. According to one source, a person's average attention span is only four seconds!

34. We don't listen efficiently; 50 to 75 per cent of most messages pass right by us. To avoid missing important information, make notes on a telephone and visitors' log as described in Chapter 6.

35. If you take a call that anyone could have handled, don't compound the time loss by obliging yourself to call back with the information. Tell the person, '*We'll* call you back on that,' and let someone else return the call once the information has been collected.

Although most people *label* the telephone as a major time-waster, used properly it can slice up to an hour or more from your day.

For one thing, it could eliminate some time-consuming appointments you might tend to make. When someone asks to see you, find out what he or she wants. The chances are you'll be able to settle it right there on the telephone.

This could apply to customers with a problem. Find out the details on the telephone. Don't go rushing to put out fires until you know all the facts. It could be that the customer, with a little guidance from you, could solve his or her own problem. Keep in mind that the customer's objective is not to see you in person, but to get out of trouble fast.

The telephone can also be used to reduce the number of letters and memos. Many letters you receive are simply asking a question or requesting some information. Resist the urge to write back. Pick up the telephone and give your answer verbally. It's usually faster, less expensive, and impresses the sender. If you need written confirmation, fine. But don't write if you don't have to.

Telemarketing

Telemarketing is now bigger than ever. As the cost of sales calls continues to increase, the telephone becomes an even more important time-saver. The head of a distribution company noted that his inside sales people were on the phone with decision-makers at least 20 hours per week. His field sales force was in face-to-face contact with decision-makers less than 14 hours per week. By training some of his more experienced field sales people in the proper use of the phone, the 50 per cent increase in contact time led to an overall 200 per cent increase in sales in two years.

If you want the telephone to work *for* you and not *against* you, you're going to have to take advantage of as many time-saving strategies as possible.

Telephone courtesy

How do you handle your *incoming* calls? Screened calls, no-nonsense dialogue, brief calls, abrupt endings may all save time, but to what end? Is saving time worth losing a customer, client or friend? We must balance our concern for time with an equal concern for others.

Don't put a caller on hold before you at least give them a chance to say a few words. Nothing is more annoying than to have a call answered with, 'Jackson Enterprises, one minute please' – followed by silence or music. What if you knew the caller was about to call you that your son was hanging from the edge of your office room by his fingertips and was slipping fast? Would you still rush back to that other call or person in your office? If you can afford the time to *answer* the phone, you can afford a few extra seconds to let callers introduce themselves before explaining that you have to put them on hold for a minute.

Similarly, if you are talking on the telephone, and another telephone rings, provide more than an abrupt 'Just a minute, please' before switching to the other caller. You have time for a brief but courteous explanation before the other phone rings three times. 'I'm sorry; the other line is ringing. Do you mind if I leave you for a moment to get their name and number?' Time being courteous is time well spent.

Many secretaries are told to ask who's calling before putting the call through. And it makes sense time-wise since it allows calls to be screened and gives you a chance to be prepared. It even affords an opportunity for the secretary to handle the minor enquiries. But be careful how it's done.

If someone asks, 'Could I speak to John Brown please?' and the immediate response is 'Could I ask who's calling?', the caller could easily get the impression he or she is being screened to see if their name is important enough to reach you. In fact, if you are tied up, and the caller is told this, the effect could be devastating. The assumption could be that you are 'tied up' because of who's calling, and that someone you considered more worthy would be put through. To avoid this, if you are actually busy on a priority project and don't want to be disturbed, don't have calls screened, have them *intercepted*. If you are busy, you are busy to *all* people, regardless of their status in or outside the organisation. By screening, you are telling the important people you are *never* busy and the unimportant people that you are *always* busy. You're impressing the wrong group! An alternative method is to have the secretary say that you are busy, but add, 'Should I interrupt her?' If it's not urgent, the chances are the caller will simply ask that you return the call. Honesty in handling incoming calls is always the best policy.

Incidentally, when *you* make a call, never force the other person's secretary to wheedle your name from you. *Announce* who's calling right at the outset. 'Hello, this is Bill Smith of Amalgamated Motors. Could I speak to John Brown, please?' This way, you will never be insulted.

Experienced authors Eugene Ehrlich and Gene Hawes urge sales people to be direct when trying to sell something: 'Telephone sales people make two big mistakes: they may act too friendly before getting down to business. They may try to disguise a sales pitch as something else. A favourite trick is to pretend they are conducting an opinion survey or are offering a free service. These are examples of bad telephone manners.'

When using the telephone to contact prospects or customers, always be polite, enthusiastic, straightforward and honest.

Car telephones

A car phone for sales people is not a luxury, but a necessity, because it helps to maximise selling time. A McGraw-Hill Research study revealed that the cost to close an industrial sale was $589.18. Furthermore, 4.3 calls were needed to close the sale, making the average cost per call $137.02. This particular study showed that sales people spent only 39 per cent of their time selling to their customers. It concluded that if having a telephone in the car could increase the average number of sales calls per day from four to five there would be a 20 per cent increase in overall effectiveness.

As technology continues to advance, a telephone in every car becomes closer to a reality. Cellular radio allows direct dialling, automatic billing, no waiting.

With the usual problems experienced by traditional car telephones eliminated (large size, poor transmission, lack of privacy, limited channel capacity etc), the mobile telephone is one more way of using driving time productively.

CHAPTER 12
Manage Your Paperwork

Coping with the paperwork explosion

Doctors have assistants to relieve them of paperwork and other routine activities so that they can spend more time in their professional income-producing practices. Other busy professionals do likewise. So why not sales people? If you are spending too much time on administrative detail and not enough time on the high pay-off, priority activities, perhaps you need an assistant. But if you have one, make sure you delegate most of the non-selling activities to him or her. As a salesperson, you should spend the bulk of your time selling. You shouldn't be spending your time answering routine letters and telephone calls, attending low-priority meetings, or searching through filing cabinets for misplaced correspondence. If you share a secretary or have access to other administrative help, take advantage of it. The general rule should be as follows:

- If it's not necessary, eliminate it.
- If it's necessary, but can be done by others, delegate it.
- If it can't be delegated, and is critical to the attainment of your objectives, do it as efficiently as possible.

Sales people are actively orientated. They like to see tangible results for their efforts. Thus they easily fall prey to unnecessary paperwork. Paperwork allows you to feel busy, takes up time, and gives you a false sense of accomplishment. It's also easier to manage than people. Spend as little time as possible on paperwork. Write only when you have to. Take short cuts. Delegate.

Force yourself to spend time on the less measurable but more valuable activities such as developing prospect lists, setting goals, planning, reading, taking sales training courses, etc.

Cutting through the avalanche of paperwork is made more difficult by the presence of photocopiers. Most copies end up in filing systems, after being shuffled from desk to desk, read and reread. Copying is so easy, and paperwork creates such an illusion of 'busyness', that it has become a national pastime. And a national time-waster. Fight it and its source – the copying machine. Control the use of copiers. Make it more difficult. Persuade management to install key-operated machines which count the number of copies made. Keys are issued to a limited number of people, who are held accountable for any abnormal increases in copies. See that there are guidelines for copier use. Determine what types of paperwork are being copied. Can you get along without copies in some cases? Try circulating a single copy instead. Let everyone know you are concerned about the proliferation of paperwork.

The habit of circulating trivial paperwork is another thorn in the side of sales people and others. Passing along junk mail, memos, reports and articles with brief, ambiguous comments such as 'for your information' and 'please handle' wastes time. Only circulate those items that you honestly feel will be of value to the person. Highlight the area you want them to note. Give specific instructions as to what they should do about the information. And tell them what to do with the paperwork afterwards (scrap, file, pass on, return etc). Communicate clearly.

Here are some tongue-in-cheek interpretations of what those brief notations on memos are actually communicating:

For your approval: ('I am passing the buck')
For your comments: ('I don't understand it myself')
For your consideration: ('I don't know what to do with it, so you hold it for a while')
Note and initial: ('Let's spread the responsibility for this')
Please expedite: ('Let's confuse them with a lot of commotion')
Please reply: ('I can't understand it, let alone answer it')
For your records: ('I'd rather clog up *your* files than mine')

For your information: ('In case I forget, I can always blame you for not taking action')

Please activate: ('Make carbon copies and add more names to the memo')

Let's get together on this: ('I assume you're as confused as I am')

Please see me regarding this: ('I want someone to talk to – it's lonely in here')

It's so easy to duplicate everything, and people have such a propensity for either filing or circulating copies, that they are becoming a salesperson's nemesis. Excess paperwork not only wastes money, it wastes time. Files and in-baskets overflow with redundant material. And the more material in the files, the harder it is to retrieve something. It may be necessary to keep certain documents, letters, reports and price lists, but is it necessary for *everyone* to keep copies of the same thing? For example, if 20 sales people all retain copies of the five-page monthly communication meeting minutes, that's 1200 pieces of paper filed annually. Multiply that by the number of different meetings, reports, memos, letters, procedures, policies, bulletins and so on that they receive in a year, and the resultant number of filed pages is unbelievable.

Encourage everyone to take action and then discard. Have specific items filed by specific people and encourage others to scrap their copies. For example, you could keep a copy of all minutes, someone else could keep a file copy of all past bulletins, another could keep a file copy of all procedures and so on – assuming that others only had to refer to them periodically. It's faster to have to refer to a central source than to shuffle through volumes of paperwork to retrieve items from a decentralised filing system. All paperwork that is referred to infrequently should be centralised. Only these items that are referred to consistently should be retained in personal files.

Reduce the volume of paperwork

In spite of electronic word processing, electronic mail, voice messaging, teleconferencing and a variety of technological developments designed to simplify communication, paperwork is still a problem. Paperwork overflows from filing cabinets and company 'paperwork morgues' to public storage firms. Business firms across Canada store some 170 million cubic feet of records. The annual cost of storing these records is about $500 million. There are stories of phenomenal cost savings through the reduction of paperwork. The annual savings resulting from the paperwork eliminated by the Canadian government during a two-year period resulted in $300 million annually. This exceeded by $100 million the target initially set for the office for the Reduction of Paperburden programme.

A frequently quoted story of Marks & Spencer illustrates what can be accomplished, with an 'if in doubt, throw it out' motto and the question, 'Would our entire business collapse if we dispensed with this?' Marks & Spencer was able to eliminate 26 million cards and sheets of paper weighing 120 tons, within one year. Both store areas and profits increased. But if technology and paper wars are really making a dent in the amount of paperwork, why are people buying so many paperclips?

Photocopies are no doubt helping to compensate for any reduced paperwork flow. It's so easy to reproduce reports, minutes and memos that most people don't give it a second thought. Why pass something around or post it or phone about it, when a touch of a button will spew out multiple copies? Kent MacDougall of the *Los Angeles Times* suggests that technology is generating more paper than ever. In addition to the role played by photocopies, he claims that 'electronic data storage makes more information available to be retrieved and presented on paper to those who need, or think they need it. And fear that a power blackout, surge or human error will wipe out the work they have entrusted to a computer induces office workers to generate paper printouts as a "back-up".'

Don't let modern technology lull you into a state of complacency. The war against paperwork must continue if we are to manage our time effectively.

Producing, storing and retrieving paperwork is time consuming. Do what you can to eliminate as much paperwork as possible.

Here are some suggestions:

1. Don't put it in writing unless absolutely necessary. Make notes in a telephone and visitors' log if you need back-up, and discard paperwork when it's no longer needed.
2. Use the telephone if the communication can be transmitted verbally. Resist the urge to write. Give verbal reports and assignments, making sure your employees note the due dates in their diaries.
3. If you produce lengthy, complicated or detailed assignments, consider recording them on cassettes. People can listen to them while they're driving, waiting, travelling etc.
4. For paperwork that must be produced and filed, record a 'throw away' date on it. Purge the files regularly and discard any outdated material.
5. Reduce the number of copies made. Send paperwork only to those people who must have it. Where time is not a factor, circulate one copy. If 10 copies are distributed, 10 copies will probably end up in the files.
6. Adhere to the motto: 'If in doubt, throw it out!' Chances are you will never have to refer to it again. If you do, you probably won't be able to find it.
7. Encourage people to respond on the original letter and return it to the sender. On your letters, stamp the words 'Save Time: Jot Your Reply Here.' On letters that you are answering, stamp the words 'Speed Reply. These notes will get the information to you faster. Please excuse the informality.'
8. Don't write follow-up letters. Send a copy of the original letter with the notation: 'Reminder. Your reply to this letter has not yet been received. Please reread this copy and let us hear from you.'
9. Discourage excessive use of the copier by assigning a key to each department. The machine will not operate without it, and will record the number of copies made.
10. Cancel all subscriptions to magazines and newsletters that are of little value, regardless of whether they are free or not.
11. Dispense with incoming paperwork the day it is received.

Don't let it accumulate. Scrap it, delegate it, answer it, or schedule a time later to answer it. The longer you leave it, the greater the likelihood of delaying it even longer. Delay breeds procrastination.

12. When reading correspondence, highlight the areas requiring an answer and dictate a reply at the time. Don't reply to thank-you letters or other correspondence that doesn't need a reply.

13. Don't play the 'paperwork game'. If junk mail is not of interest to you, it will probably not be of interest to others in your company. Resist the urge to circulate it with vague notations such as 'Please note' or 'For your information'.

14. Keep your letters brief. Be clear, concise and simple. Limit your letters to one page. You not only save paper, your letter is more likely to get read the moment it's received.

15. When running copies of reports, minutes etc, back up the pages and use double-sided copying to cut the number of pages by half.

Handle your mail efficiently

In spite of your efforts to reduce the volume of paperwork, you will still have plenty to handle. Do it efficiently. Don't be intimidated by the volume that descends upon you. Most of it can be dispensed with quickly.

If you receive a lot of useless unsolicited mail, it's usually because you're subscribing to a lot of magazines that sell their mailing lists to direct-mail houses. If that's the case, use a special code, such as a phoney middle initial, when you subscribe to magazines. Then a secretary can screen out all the envelopes and other literature bearing that code.

On the other hand, if you're receiving a lot of valuable money-saving and time-saving ideas from the 'junk mail', it may pay you to spend time on it. Not all unsolicited mail is useless. Everything is a time trade-off. If experience reveals that the value received outweighs the time spent, and the time spent does not steal time from priority tasks, then peruse all junk mail. Everyone's situation is not the same. So don't let 'experts' convince you to do something that's not right for your situation.

Did you read about the man who got on every conceivable mailing list so he would receive enough junk mail to heat his house? It seems he burns it at night in his wood stove. Most of us would not go this far to solicit junk mail, but we do have plenty to contend with, and if we threw it away, unseen, we'd miss many good ideas. So streamline your handling of junk mail so that you can deal with it quickly. Glance at it, but don't read every word. Search for ideas, marking those of interest with a yellow highlighter pen. Store potential ideas in an 'ideas file' and review them one week later. If some do seem like good ideas, do something about them. Otherwise, scrap the file. Don't let the junk mail accumulate.

If you are confident that someone else is able to identify the items that interest you, you could have the junk mail screened. Otherwise, deal with it quickly yourself. Never circulate it to other people to waste *their* time unless you *know* it will be of interest to them. 'When in doubt, throw it out' is still a reasonable guideline.

One American executive has his secretary separate incoming paperwork into five folders as follows: red for 'hot' (to be read immediately); orange for material that needs his attention today; yellow for what has to be read this week; white for weekend reading; and black for documents requiring his signature.

Although five folders may be more than necessary, it takes very little time to slip the various items into different folders rather than lump them all together into one. And priority items can be dealt with quickly without sorting through – and being distracted by – items of lesser importance.

Here are some ways to streamline the flow of paperwork:

1. Don't work on your mail on and off throughout the day. Schedule a definite time each day to dispense with all of it. At that time either scrap it, delegate it, do it, or schedule a time to do it later.
2. Don't be tempted to look at paperwork when it's dropped in your in-tray. Interrupting yourself with paperwork will decrease your efficiency.

3. If someone opens your mail for you, ask them to sort it into three folders marked 'priority', 'routine' and 'junk mail'. Work on it in that order.
4. Keep paperwork out of sight in a follow-up file until you're ready to work on it, otherwise it will distract you from the job at hand.
5. Use form letters where possible. Also have 'model' letters available to use for reference so that you don't have to continually compose new ones for similar situations.
6. Photocopying instead of using carbon copies eliminates the necessity of correcting copies as well as the original. Photocopying also retains the letterhead.
7. Fold your letters so that the letterhead is revealed and the reader will be able to spot your ideas quickly.
8. When sorting correspondence internally, use coloured envelopes to identify priority items.
9. When editing copy for retyping, use a different colour so that the markings will stand out.
10. Consider letting the typist or secretary proofread your letters to that you need only to sign them.
11. When composing long letters, itemise and number the ideas; this saves time in writing, reading and replying.
12. Reply to routine letters by making notes on the original and returning it.
13. Keep your letters brief. Short letters get read first.
14. Add a postscript if you realise that you omitted some important information. Don't retype the letter unless absolutely necessary.
15. Use headings such as 'Widget Analysis' on your letters. It's easier to file, and lets your reader know right away what the letter is about.

CHAPTER 13
The Power of Positive Reading

Effective reading

If you read one book every week, you will still only be reading about one-fifth of 1 per cent of the books being published. Speed-reading courses alone are not enough to allow you to cope with the information explosion. You must be selective in what you read, take advantage of book reviews, and subscribe to book summary services. Skim books, highlight key information, and extract those ideas which will help you achieve your personal and organisational goals.

You should also home in on those subjects of greatest interest and benefit. Ask someone to review publishers' catalogues for relevant titles. Ask your friends to refer books and magazine articles to you. And do the same for them. You may find it worthwhile to subscribe to a newsclipping service in order to obtain articles on specific topics as they appear in magazines and newspapers. You might also alert bookstores and libraries to your area of interest.

Sales people spend over 13 hours per week reading business-related material. Every year the amount of reading we are required to do seems to increase. Yet our reading speed remains the same. This produces a backlog. We either have to absorb more in the same time or be more selective in what we read – perhaps both.

To maintain our effectiveness we must keep up to date. We can't ignore the thousands of books, magazines and technical papers being published every year. But neither can we read indiscriminately. Time is too precious. Here are some hints on tackling the problem.

Be selective

There are about 50,000 books published in Britain every year; you certainly can't read them *all*. James T McCay in his book, *The Management of Time*, suggests you can read 50,000 words per minute. All you have to do is recognise within one minute that a 50,000-word book is not going to help you, and then don't read it.

How long do you spend reading newspapers? Some people subscribe to as many as three or four faily or weekly newspapers, and actually spend time with all of them. Even though they cover the same news! Some of the news is worth reading, but there's so much other material that 'catches the eye' the cost in time is phenomenal. The important news is also carried on the radio, television and in weekly news magazines, so all that exposure may not really be necessary. It's important to be kept up to date on what's going on in the world, but don't spend more time than is necessary. Take a hard look at the newspapers and magazines you receive – with a view to eliminating most of them.

Don't let unwanted material intrude on your time. If you currently receive magazines which offer no value, cancel your subscription. Come off the mailing list. Resist the temptation to accept them simply because they're free. Read only those magazines and books which will help you to attain your personal and organisational goals. A good guideline is to review only those publications which consistently publish relevant articles. One or two useful articles per year is not sufficient payback for your time invested.

One company has controlled the magazine explosion by intercepting all magazines at the reception area, eliminating all duplications (by contacting the publisher) and filing one copy of each magazine in the company library. Then each month a list of the magazines received is sent to the staff. They request, through one person, any magazine they want to see. The company claims it has eliminated the time-wasting impulse people have of browsing through all magazines, useful or otherwise.

An alternative method is to have only the 'contents' pages circulated. Then everyone can indicate which specific articles they are interested in, eliminating the necessity of sending the whole magazine. Copies of the requested articles are then sent to the various individuals.

Handle magazines quickly

If you must screen your own magazines, don't retain them. Tear out the articles of interest, punch them, staple the pages together, and insert them into a folder marked 'READ'. If the magazine must be circulated, photocopy the articles instead. Don't actually read the articles until later. Carry the 'READ' folder in your briefcase and refer to it during idle times while waiting for clients on your flight to leave or while standing in queues.

When you read any articles, books or business reports, keep a highlighter pen in your hand. When you read something useful, mark it. After you've read the entire article, go back and review those marked areas. Put everything you can into practice right away. Copy the rest on to index cards or A4 sheets of paper and put them into your 'ideas' file for future reference.

If entire paragraphs or articles are full of useful ideas and information, simply place a vertical mark in the margin running the length of the paragraph. Do not use the article as a colouring book.

Once you've read a book, article, business report etc, you shouldn't have to reread it or refer to pertinent parts. They should be permanently marked for easy reference. It saves time.

Your articles, once read, marked and acted upon, should be filed in ring binders. Identify binder contents by pasting a picture of some representative symbol on the spine (such as a clock for 'time') along with the appropriate word; this helps to make identification easier.

The 'ultimate' in storing magazines is to have them bound in hard cover, like an encyclopedia. You can have from 24 to 36 magazines to a 'volume', with title and dates on the spine for easy identification on a book shelf. Have different-coloured bindings for different magazines. No more searching through stacks of magazines or shelves. No more 'missing issues'. No dog-eared pages or torn magazines. A real time-saver. Only for good reference magazines, though – ones you would keep on your shelf in your library. The publishers often sell the binders.

Read actively

The average reading speed is only 230 to 250 words per minute, but you can scan literature at 1000 to 5000 words per minute. Don't simply absorb whatever information hits your eye. Search out the information you require.

The title should tell you what the article is about. Turn it into a question and actively search for the answers. For example, if the article is entitled, 'How to save time at meetings', change it to read 'How can I save time at meetings?' and search for those ways. Keep a highlighter in your hand and mark those sentences which provide the information you're looking for. By reading with a purpose, your mind will not wander and you'll cover the material more quickly.

If sales people spend an average of 13 hours per week reading business-related material, a 10 per cent improvement in reading speed will yield over an hour per week.

Read faster

At reading speeds of 250 words per minute, the average for most people, getting through the million-words a week requirement of executives would take $66\frac{1}{2}$ working hours. Take a speed reading course if you have the time. But you can more than double your speed without it. Simply push yourself. Don't vocalise, even to yourself. And don't review words or sentences you miss. It's the ideas that are important. Don't try to read every word. Search out the ideas, mark them with that highlighter, and keep on going. Use your peripheral vision to its fullest. Take in as many words as possible at one glance. You can practise this by reading a newspaper column with your eyes moving in a downward direction only. The column is narrow enough to take in at one glance without moving from side to side. If you are an active reader, consciously read as fast as possible; concentration will be easier. You won't have time to daydream or yield to distractions. And the faster you read, the better you'll understand.

Handle books the same way

Inspect the contents page, read the preface and introduction. Examine the first and last chapters and, assuming the book is relevant, read it as you would a magazine article. Use the highlighter. Make marginal notes (assuming it's not someone else's book). Don't bury those ideas by replacing the book on the shelf. Review it quickly, dictating those ideas you marked for transcribing on to 3- × 5-inch index cards. Or photocopy relevant pages and include them in the appropriate binder, along with the magazine articles. Whether it's magazines, books, or other literature, it's imperative that you pick out the profitable ideas and put them into action – or into an easily accessible file. Don't get into the habit of rereading articles or book chapters later. It's a waste of time.

Take advantage of time-savers

To save time scanning books, subscribe to book-summary guides and scan book review columns in business papers and magazines. Take advantage of abstract services.

Newsletters are a good source of condensed, current information and are available for almost every conceivable subject from computers to housekeeping. There are over 100 books currently available which address the topic of time management alone. This illustrates the value of newsletters. Books are not always bursting with ideas, and it would take a lot of time to dig out enough ideas to fill a newsletter. Investigate the newsletters available. It would be wise to subscribe to those that relate directly to your profession.

CHAPTER 14
How to Say 'No'

It's so *easy* to say 'Yes' when asked to tackle a new job or additional responsibility. In fact, you receive immediate rewards – you feel a sense of satisfaction, a feeling of self-worth; and you receive praise and gratitude from the other person. But it's short-lived. It's replaced by a feeling of panic and pressure, a sense of hopelessness that you have taken on more than you can possibly handle.

Why don't we say 'No' more often? Part of the reason is that we want to be liked. Respected. Admired. It's good for our feeling of self-worth. It's a warm feeling to be able to do things for other people. It's good to be needed!

But look at the price we have to pay. Stress. Worry. A sense of urgency. Illness precipitated by excessive demands on our time.

It takes self-discipline to say 'No', but it's worth it. So force yourself to say 'No' more often. It becomes easier the more you say it. Don't worry about not being liked. What do *you* think of someone who agrees to everything and then never delivers? It's better to decline now than to let somebody down later.

Don't provide a long 'excuse' when you say 'No'. If you qualify a negative reply with a statement such as 'I really don't think I'm qualified, or I'd do it', they'll convince you that you are qualified. Or if you say you don't have time, they'll tell you how *little* time it really takes. Simply say, 'No, I can't, but I appreciate your asking me,' and leave it at that. You don't owe anybody a long drawn-out explanation.

Many of us find it difficult to say 'No' when turned to for help because we feel our reasons for *not* agreeing to take on the task might not be convincing enough. We don't want people to resent us or lose respect for us. And saying 'No' seems so distasteful that it's easier to do the job than risk alienation. It's more *comfortable* at the time to say 'Yes'.

But the same is true for a lot of things. Think how painful it was to stand up in front of a class to give a five-minute speech; or introduce yourself to a stranger at a party; or speak up at a meeting; or make that first sales call. Yet most of us have overcome our fear of such situations. And we can overcome our fear of saying 'No' in the same way – by forcing ourselves to do it. Again and again. Until our fear dissipates to a feeling of discomfort. It will never be enjoyable – or shouldn't be, because we are disappointing someone – but it will be tolerable and not upsetting. By saying 'No' more often to the activities which we shouldn't be involved in, we are able to spend more time on those meaningful activities which will help us to reach our goals.

If someone asks you to serve on a committee, and you cannot afford the time, nor can you see any benefit from it, don't hesitate. Don't give the impression you are considering it. Say 'No' immediately. Provide a *brief* explanation if you feel one is necessary. Do not offer long, drawn-out complicated reasons that make it look as though you're searching for excuses.

We are so used to doing favours for people and agreeing to requests, that we say 'Yes' even if doing so doesn't make sense. Next time, don't be so quick to say 'Yes'. Think first. Is the request reasonable? Is it going to interfere with your own work? Is it compatible with your goals? Perhaps you *should* say 'Yes' – but at least assess the request before agreeing to it.

You may *want* to say 'Yes' to some requests – the ones that relate to your long-term or short-term goals. But you may have to get out of other commitments before you take on new ones. Explain that you couldn't take on that task right now, but you would like to in the future once you free yourself from other obligations. If they need an answer immediately, don't take any chances – say 'No'. It's easy to change your mind later and say 'Yes'. But look how hard it is to say 'No' once you've already committed yourself with a 'Yes'!

Those future commitments can be your downfall, so don't say

'Yes' to something just because it's in the future. It's easy to get coerced because you don't feel the immediate time pressure, but the chances are, when it's time to fulfil those future commitments, you'll be up to your eyes in activities. Only say 'Yes' if you *know* you will be less busy when the time comes to do the task (which is unlikely). If you have no reason to think you will be any less busy in the future, treat it as though it *were* now, and say 'No'.

What if you *boss* asks you to do something? Well, that certainly relates to your goals – if employment is one of them. But if you schedule your tasks properly, you'll never *have* to say 'No' to the boss. Simply show your planning diary and explain that there's no time now, *unless* the boss would like to juggle priorities, and delay some of those tasks and sales calls that you have scheduled.

Recognise that you cannot do everything or be all things to all people. Accept those activities which will further your organisational and personal goals. Then don't take on any new ones, unless they are more important than those you are already working on. Even then, they should *displace* something, not add to it.

Sometimes it's easier to say 'No' if you don't have your planning diary with you. If you have it with you when someone asks if you're available on a certain date, the tendency is to flip it open, admit that it appears to be free, and book the appointment. But the appointment may be extremely low priority in comparison to other projects you are working on. You should take time to consider the other jobs you have on the go before committing yourself – even though at the moment it may seem expedient and polite to acquiesce.

If you don't have your planner in sight, explain that you will have to check your diary and get back to them. This will give you the opportunity to assess your workload and priorities before responding. Your reply might turn out to be, 'Sorry, Pete, I've checked my schedule and its virtually impossible to meet you next week'.

The solution might be to keep your planner in your briefcase, and a *notebook* in your pocket or handbag. Use the notebook to jot down the reminder to check your planner. But operate as though your planner were back at the office.

Most of us have a problem saying 'No' to people, and we realise we must be more assertive or we'll be spending a lifetime responding to the demands of others. But there's another problem. We frequently can't say 'No' to ourselves, either. So we stop for a coffee, read the newspaper before we make that first call, drop into the snack bar, procrastinate . . . We must also say 'No' to ourselves more often if we are going to manage our time successfully.

CHAPTER 15
Twenty-five Time Tips

The key to effective selling is to spend your time where it will do the most good. This involves a continuing evaluation of your present customers to determine which ones offer increasing sales potential, which are steady but valuable, and which are declining.

Spend more time on high-potential customers and look for replacements for the declining ones. Don't fall victim to the 80/20 rule, where you spend 80 per cent of your time on customers who only account for 20 per cent of your sales.

You may have to spend over 15 per cent of your time cultivating new prospects just to stay ahead of customer attrition. Make that time count. Keep a good prospect file with all the useful information you can get on each prospect – information that will help you sell to him or her.

It's claimed that 80 per cent of the sales are made on the first call, 23 per cent on the second, and only 7 per cent on the third. Why do most sales people spend so much time chasing only 7 per cent? Depending on your industry, you might be wasting your time on low-return sales calls.

One of the highest pay-off areas for effective time management is in sales. Face-to-face selling accounts for less than 30 per cent of a salesman's time. The other areas, according to a report, were as follows:

Travel	30%
Prospecting for new accounts	5%
Writing reports and collecting data	10–12%
Administrative tasks	7%

Waiting to see accounts	3%
Telephone work	10%
Entertaining	7%

There's nothing unique about a salesperson's time problem. At least 70 per cent of their time is spent on the same kinds of activity as managers. The challenge in sales is (1), to increase the amount of selling time by becoming more effective in the other areas, and (2), to use the selling time wisely. After all, they could be trying to sell to the wrong people. Or spending too much time with low-value accounts.

Most sales people spend less than one-third of their day in actual face-to-face selling. They can increase the amount of selling time by being organised, setting goals, planning each day in advance, setting priorities, controlling lunch times and idle times, conserving travel time, and taking advantage of as many time-saving ideas as possible.

Here is a summary of time tips for individuals involved in selling:

1. Set goals. Determine how much business you want to do. Budget the time to do it. If you spend 20 hours a week face-to-face with customers, one of your goals may be to increase that to 25 or 30 hours.
2. Make a daily list of critical calls to make and things to do; assign a priority to each; work on only one item at a time, starting with the most important.
3. Start early; much paperwork or planning can be completed before 9 am. Also, some customers prefer receiving callers early. Always reserve prime working hours for your most important personal sales calls.
4. Evaluate critically whether each sales call or trip is really necessary. Can its purpose be accomplished as effectively by telephone or letter?
5. Prepare fully before each call or trip. Make sure you take everything you'll need with you; use a checklist. Conserve travel time; maximise sales calls per trip; preplan routing to minimise travel and backtracking. Avoid driving between

calls in congested areas; save time by walking or by taking a taxi or bus. Plan your day in advance; don't stop halfway through and try to decide which calls to make next.

6. Be *on time* for all sales calls. Being late is unforgivable. Being early is a waste of time and makes you look too eager. A good idea is to allow more time than necessary to get there, and spend the extra time in your car or in the reception area doing priority paperwork. Use waiting time productively: review sales presentations, handle routine chores, plan or phone ahead. Place limits on waiting time; make a new appointment for another time and leave. If it's about an urgent matter, telephone later.

7. When travelling out of town, stay overnight where you'll be working the next day. You can then start the day fresh and early after reviewing sales call plans and preparations the evening before.

8. Respect your customer's time. It is just as valuable to him or her as it is to you. Be prepared, be organised, be brief and congenial. But don't apologise for taking his or her time. You're there to benefit their company. Control sales interview time. Some friendly conversation is always constructive, but don't waste customer's time or let them waste yours.

9. Control lunch times – especially when entertaining customers. Long, congenial lunches often prove less productive than short office calls; they may even ruin the rest of the day for other saleswork.

10. Be creative. Audio visual units, charts, slides etc, may save presentation time and be more effective. Don't be afraid to try something new.

11. Log the amount of time you spend with each customer. Beware of spending too much time with those warm, friendly customers who make you feel good, waste your time, and buy very little. What counts is not whether you like a customer, but how much business that customer may generate. Your best bet is to call on the high-value accounts or prospects first. Spending time with those safe, sure, friendly accounts that buy very little makes you feel good,

but it also prevents you from developing accounts that buy more.

12. Some customers are too demanding and steal your time away from more valuable customers. There's a limit to the price you can afford to pay in order to maintain a customer. If they get too demanding, you may have to take a firm stand.

13. Eliminate casual goodwill calls; visit customers only when you have something constructive to discuss.

14. Time spent evaluating each sales call is time well spent. What went wrong? What went right? How could you improve on it the next time? No matter how good you are, one of your goals should be to get better. We learn from our experiences only if we remember them and take corrective action.

15. Make appointments in advance whenever possible. This helps to ensure that your contact will be available when you arrive and reduces time lost in fruitless travel. When making appointments, make sure you have established the ending time as well as the starting time of your meeting in advance. Plan to work within that time frame. If customers respect you and your habits, they'll respect your product or service. Estimate the time sales calls will take and don't run over time. Respect your own time and your customer's time.

16. While you're with the customer, set a time and date for the next call while the customer's diary is relatively clear.

17. Always telephone before leaving the office to keep an appointment; it may prevent a wasted trip. People frequently forget to record appointments in their office planners – and sometimes they record them but forget to check their diaries.

18. To prevent loss of productive time when a customer cancels an appointment at the last minute, always have alternative calls tentatively scheduled.

19. To keep track of the cost of business lunches and dinners that are tax-deductible, jot down the details on your credit card receipt at the time you sign it. This will prevent you from forgetting later. A daily expense diary is also a good idea – and a timesaver.

20. Reduce paperwork to a bare minimum. Handle these during time that is least productive for personal selling. Use a 31-day

follow-up file to help remember things to be done on specific future dates. But review it regularly; don't lose things in it.

21. Keep your car in good running condition. Fill up with petrol during 'off hours'.

22. Keep physically fit. Take holidays. Be at your peak during prime selling time.

23. Take your breaks during idle time. Don't steal valuable selling time by stopping for a coffee and a review of the latest stock-market quotations.

24. Keep a daily diary of your activities. Record all information that you feel may be useful later. Don't rely on your memory.

25. Be determined to practise self-discipline, avoid tempting time-wasters (such as socialising with friendly, low-value prospects) and work towards a predetermined set of daily, weekly and monthly goals.

CHAPTER 16
Manage Your Life

Be life-conscious

Not only should we not *waste* our lives, we should not simply *spend* our lives either. Life is too short to be treated so casually. We should *invest* our lives in those things that have lasting value.

Assume you had paid £100 per hour, in advance, for whatever time you have remaining on this earth. Would you waste it foolishly? I doubt it. Yet, because we have received life as a gift, we unconsciously treat it as though it were of low value. In actual fact, it is priceless.

We must not simply become time-conscious; we must become life-conscious. Being time-conscious might involve cramming as many activities as possible into an hour. And it could be equivalent to spending £100 on dozens of pieces of worthless junk. Being life-conscious involves recognising the priceless nature of time, and investing it wisely in high-return activities and projects.

Recognise time for what it is; not something to be squandered, but something to be used wisely.

How often does someone exclaim, 'I just have to get this done!', while doggedly working bleary-eyed into the late evening. Nothing *has* to get done, although there might be big consequences if it's not. But what *are* the consequences of doing that task? And what price are you paying in order to get it done?

Mr Stan Mooneyham, President of World Vision International, related the following story:

'A traveller was making a long journey by train in a foreign country. He put his valise on the overhead rack, and having been warned to guard his bag at all times against thieves, he looked frequently at the rack.

'Darkness fell, lights were turned on, the train clattered through the night. The traveller did not dare sleep; he had to watch his valise. By morning, he was bleary-eyed, but he had kept awake; his valise was secure. Keeping his eyes open became torture, and despite his valiant efforts, they closed for a few moments. With a start, he awoke and looked up. The valise was gone. "Thank God," he sighed, "now I can go to sleep!".'

Most things seem important until something *more* important comes along. In the above story, sleep was the real priority. And in our own situation as sales people, rest and relaxation might also be more important than working far into the night. We might have to sacrifice an immediate return by ignoring a task, but would be in a better state of mind to create even higher pay-back ideas after getting our necessary quota of sleep.

Question everything you do. Does it justify the expenditure of time, energy and money necessary to complete it? The answer may be 'Yes'. And perhaps nothing of importance is being sacrificed in order to do it. But at least recognise that most things are relative, and that questioning everything you do will ensure that you are working on the real priority.

Concentrate on results, not activity

It's easy to become comfortable with 'busyness'. Jumping from one job to another, one meeting to another, while spewing out paperwork, provides us with a sense of accomplishment and tangible evidence of activity. But how effective are we? The less a person has to do in order to produce results, the more effective he or she is.

We live in an activity-orientated world, and it's easy to get caught up in the bustle. We take alternate routes when traffic is heavy, even though we would travel less actual distance and arrive at the same time if we had stayed put. The movement gives us a feeling of progress. We walk up stairs when lifts are slow, make a second trip to the bank rather than wait in the queue, and even try to finish someone else's sentence when they pause during a conversation.

Similarly, we will walk to someone's office instead of using the intercom, only to find out they are already tied up. We walk to the copying machine each time we need something copied instead of allowing it to accumulate or leaving it for someone else. We shout across the office instead of telephoning. We make six return trips to the secretary during the day instead of making a single trip in the afternoon. We deliver mail in person, write unnecessary letters, and phone some people six or more times a day.

Realise that the name of the game is accomplishment, not activity. Think ahead. It's better to wait than to move needlessly. At least the waiting time can be effectively used on something else. Activity for activity's sake is a time-waster. Thinking is more productive than walking aimlessly; planning is more effective than trial and error doing, and eliminating an unnecessary task is more important than swift, efficient performance.

Our approach to our jobs and to our lives should be one of working and living smarter, not harder. Modifying our sense of urgency and our penchant for activity and directing this energy towards goal-setting, planning, and creative thinking, can increase our productivity, decrease stress, make us more valuable to our organisations, and more available to our families.

Give some people a thousand pounds and they'll multiply it tenfold through effective money management. Give the same people something of even greater value – a thousand hours – and they squander it on meaningless activities. Don't be one of those irresponsible spendthrifts. Manage your time well. You will be rewarded by selling more in less time – and living more *all* the time!

Bibliography

Time management

Bender, James F. *How to Sell Well*, McGraw-Hill, 1971

Bliss, Edwin. *Getting Things Done*, Futura, 1985

Douglass, Merrill E and Donna N Douglass. *Manage Your Time, Manage your Work, Manage Yourself*, AMACOM, 1980

Drucker, Peter F. *The Effective Executive*, Pan 1970; Heinemann 1982

Hill, Napoleon. *Think and Grow Rich*, Wilshire, 1970

Knaus, William J. *Do It Now: How to Stop Procrastinating*, Prentice-Hall, 1979

Lakein, Alan. *How to Get Control of Your Time and Your Life*, Gower, 1985

Le Boeuf, Michael. *Working Smart: How to Accomplish More in Half the Time*, McGraw-Hill, 1979

McCay, James T. *The Management of Time*, Prentice-Hall, 1974

Mackenzie, Alec. *The Time Trap*, AMACOM, 1972

Mackenzie, Alec and Kay Cronkite Waldo, *About Time! A Woman's Guide to Time Management*, McGraw-Hill, 1981

Reynolds, Helen and Mary E Tramel. *Executive Time Management: Getting 12 Hours' Work out of an 8-Hour Day*, Prentice-Hall, 1979

Seiwert, Lothar J. *Managing Your Time*, Kogan Page, 1989

Seiwert, Lothar J. *Time is Money – Save It*, Kogan Page, 1991

Taylor, Harold L. *What's Your Time Worth?* and *Further Up the Organisation*, Hodder and Stoughton, 1985

Winston, Stephanie. *The Organised Executive*, Kogan Page, 1989

Further reading from Kogan Page

Don't Do. Delegate!, J M Jenks and J M Kelly, 1986
Readymade Business Forms, Michael Armstrong, 1991
Readymade Business Letters, Jim Dening, 1988
Readymade Business Speeches, Barry Turner, 1989

Sales and marketing titles
The Best Seller, D Forbes Ley, 1988
Cold Calling Techniques, Stephan Schiffman, 1989
How to Increase Sales Without Leaving Your Desk, Edmund Tirbutt, 1991
Multi-Level Marketing, Peter Clothier, 1990
Selling by Telephone, Len Rogers, 1986
Selling to Win, Richard Denny, 1989